I SPY SOMETHING!

A PRACTICAL GUIDE TO CLASSROOM OBSERVATIONS OF YOUNG CHILDREN

Ann Marie Leonard, Ph.D.

SOUTHERN EARLY CHILDHOOD ASSOCIATION

Southern Early Childhood Association
P.O. Box 55930
Little Rock, AR 72215-5930

The names of all children and families in this book have been changed to
protect their privacy.

The Southern Early Childhood Association provides a variety of publications,
videos, and symposia for teachers and care givers of young children. For more
information about our services, write, call, or e-mail us at SECA@aristotle.net.

SECA makes every effort to assure that developmentally appropriate practices
and cultural diversity are depicted throughout our publications, products, and
materials. The opinions expressed in this book, however, are those of the
author(s) and not necessarily of SECA and/or its affiliates.

ISBN 0-942388-24-0

Printed in the United States of America
by A.C.H. Graphics   tel. 1-501-753-6113

-Table of Contents-

Photo Credits:

page 5—**Nancy P. Alexander**   page 22—**Subjects & Predicates**   page 55—**Nancy P. Alexande**
page 7—**Nancy P. Alexander**   page 25—**Sally P. Evitt**   page 64—**Subjects & Predicates**
page 8—**Andrea Robinson**   page 30—**Nancy P. Alexander**   page 71—**Sally P. Evitt**
page 11—**Francis Wardle**   page 39—**Subjects & Predicates**   page 78—**Francis Wardle**
page 19—**Francis Wardle**   page 44—**Nancy P. Alexander**

-Preface-

More than 20 years ago, when I began working with undergraduate students preparing to teach young children, this book was first conceived. I was assigned a child development course that was designed to teach the content through students' first-hand observations of young children. What a novel idea! I soon discovered that if a student didn't already have well-developed observational abilities, the experience was a total loss. Clearly, the first step was to develop keen observation skills in my students. I set out looking for ways to achieve that task.

In the infancy period of this book's development, I worked on defining observation tools and searching for observational methods in the professional literature. I thought surely somebody knew it all, and I just needed to find what they had written. Searching helped me find how other people worked with observation and the tools they used, but I never found that one book that would meet the needs of my students. At the same time, I began to trust that observation skills held great potential for teachers as they worked to improve their teaching effectiveness.

As the book's concept became a toddler, I experimented as a toddler does with language. What words gave an observation concept the best chance to be understood by a novice observer? Autonomy is a big thing for toddlers, and so it was for me at this stage of thinking about observation skills. I needed to find my own way and make my own decisions, which I did.

To continue the analogy from a developmental perspective, the book's preschool years were ones of having ideas and doing something about them. My sense of initiative was at work. How those observation skills might be implemented was a big theme. To what other situations might those observation tools be applied? I constantly looked for how to reconcile new ideas with my ideas.

Well, when this developing book reached the school-age years, I struggled with issues of competence. New handouts for students, new ways to demonstrate the applicability of observation skills, and the various tools for teachers and questions of their effectiveness were constantly being addressed.

The rebellious struggle for this book's identity seemed to coincide with the movement against standardized testing and toward authentic assessment. The role of observation changed directions, or at least the justification for it changed, in the eyes of many educators. Observation skills became part of the critical competencies needed by teachers to effectively engage in authentic assessment of children's progress. Teacher observations became legitimized as part of the portfolio assessment movement. Ah! A real identity!

So now after all this development, the book concept now in its early twenties has reached a level of maturity. Its content reflects a level of confidence and a recognition of the identity and status observation skills must be afforded if we are to be effective teachers, especially well-prepared teachers of young children.

Several VIP's have had great influence on my understanding of the importance and application of observation skills over the years. Among them are: Mrs. Mildred Dickerson, a past president of SACUS, now SECA, and my long-time mentor, colleague, and friend; Jimmy Hymes, who helped me see that writing to the audience is a good thing; Betty Rowen, author of *The Children We See*, who introduced me to many observation concepts; all the college students in my observation-based courses over the years who have been my eyes for continuing to learn about children and vicariously helped me refine my observation skills; and most of all the children I have had the pleasure of knowing through observation.

Special thanks are due to my patient and understanding husband, George Merz, to Jan McCracken, who read the manuscript in midstream and made great suggestions, and especially to Chrissy Leister-Willis for her patience, understanding, and believing that this book needed to be published.

—Ann Marie Leonard

-Introduction-

Why Become a Keen Observer of Children?

Each day as we work with children, their actions provide clues to help us understand how life is going for them. We can learn a great deal by paying attention to what they do and say. Their actions provide a window to their person. A written record of what they say and do helps us think about and remember what we have observed through that window.

I Spy Something! will help you improve your skills for observing and recording young children's actions. Like learning to ride a bicycle, developing the skills of objective observation takes time, effort, and much practice! After you become a keen observer, these skills will become a part of who you are and how you think. You will find that you are more observant of your own world, and each day will be in sharper focus for you.

"Convince me that I should work that hard," you say? "Why should I expend the time, effort, and energy to become a keen observer?" The benefits for teachers, children, and families fall into several categories.

1. Observation helps us get to know children as individuals with unique personalities. Each child is a unique individual with special qualities which define that uniqueness. Children are the sum total of all their experiences, including their culture and all their inherited characteristics. No two children are *EVER* the same. We have to figure out *who they are* as well as *what it is* that makes them who they are.

In the preschool program I coordinate, we were fortunate to work with a pair of identical twins. On first glance, we couldn't tell which was Elly and which was Sally. As we observed and got to know them, we discovered how very different they were as individuals. One was almost always positive, while the other saw the limitations. One was a confident risk-taker, while the other needed adult encouragement to try new things. One consistently considered others, while the other was typically concerned with the impact of actions on herself. We had to observe them in action to know which one was Elly and which one was Sally.

2. Information acquired through observation helps us base educational decisions on the children in our classrooms. What you learn about children through careful observation will help you be a more effective teacher. Good teaching decisions require that we know and understand each child as an individual, as a member of a culture, and as one person within an age group. The child-sensitive, caring teacher is concerned with helping all children reach their potential within the context of group interactions. That happens most effectively when teachers know and understand each child's starting point and recognize the subtleties of change.

Twins Elly and Sally illustrate this point quite well also. For Elly, having the paper, glue, and glitter on the table was all that was necessary for her to create a masterpiece. Not so for Sally. She needed convincing that she could do it without help and wasn't going to make a mistake. Sally needed someone to show her how to hold the glue container and what it could do. Sally needed someone to assure her that we appreciated her creation and that her mom would be pleased.

When Carl, another of our four-year-olds looked at a forsythia blossom and said, "This is a four-sythia. If it had three petals, it would be a three-sythia. If it had two petals, it would be a two-sythia, and one petal, it would be a one-sythia." By observing and noting what Carl told us, we realized we needed to add new challenges to the math activities in our classroom and that Carl was thinking and reasoning at a level beyond many of the other children.

3. Observation helps us understand what children know and are learning. It is the first and best approach for assessment. Young children aren't good test takers. They don't sit well or follow test-type instructions well. Just like adults, they often speak words they don't understand. All of these characteristics mean that to know and recognize what children really know and what they are learning requires another assessment strategy. A variety of observation strategies and tools will improve your ability to really *know* what children understand and what they have learned.

Observation is the first and most authentic tool for assessing young children's learning and development.

4. Enhanced observation skills enrich our personal lives and broaden our understanding of the world, ourselves, and others. One personal advantage of enhanced observation skills is our ability to see and be aware of the wants, issues, and concerns of all the people we know. Life is fuller and richer when we include others.

We all miss opportunities to respond to others when we don't observe carefully. Young children don't often ask, they act. Tuning in to children's actions will help you know when they are in need. When children receive our attention without having to ask, we communicate that we care. Good observation skills help us know when and how to provide that attention.

Through our observations of others, we have the opportunity to see how alike we all are as people, and to recognize how different we are as individuals. There is something encouraging in our realization that others struggle with many of the same issues, concerns, and problems. Usually only the evidence of our struggles looks different.

5. Observation data provides important raw material for us to help families see and understand their child's progress. We have all faced that difficult conference with families who aren't going to be happy with what we need to tell them. Children need families to be their unconditional advocates. That role sometimes makes families skeptical of what teachers have to say. Particularly in those cases, actual dates, times, frequencies, and circumstances to support our ideas about their child are essential for our message to be believed. More positively, what a joy it is to a family for their child's teacher to share the triumphs and progress with that same care and attention to detail.

Peter's mom came in for a conference with his second grade teacher. All the observation information his teacher had gathered pointed toward a vision problem. Peter's mom was adamant that he couldn't possibly have a vision problem because he'd just been screened before entering first grade. When his teacher described in detail what she had seen, the impact on his school work, and the frequency (dates, number of occurrences, and the time of day) of his behavior, his mom began to listen more objectively.

Two weeks later when Peter came to school wearing new glasses, the teacher received a note from his mom. It went something like this: ⇨

> The power of objective information acquired through observation is an important ally. Dates, frequencies, and the time of observations are also critical in situations where families don't see the same behavior at home. Observation-based information is always important when communicating with families about their child.

> Dear Mrs. B.,
>
> Thank you for all your efforts to convince me to take my son to the eye doctor. Dr. M. found some major vision problems which he was able to correct. He was amazed that Peter was able to function at all at school. I wouldn't have believed his vision could be the problem without your information. Peter hasn't been the same since his father died last year. I thought his problems at school were just a continuation of that. I'm so glad he has such a caring teacher and that you took the time to try to figure out how to help him. I can't thank you enough.
>
> Sincerely,
> Mrs. James

*   *   *

Here are some special considerations for adults who work with children during the early childhood years. Consider the implications that describe the age level of children with whom you work or plan to work. Consider these characteristics of children as you think about observing them.

- Adults who nurture **infants and toddlers** must be highly sensitive to and skilled in reading nonverbal cues. Infants and toddlers are language beginners. Using words to share ideas is not a strength for this age group.
- Adults who nurture **preschool children** must build observation skills because this is a period of many changes in their skills and capabilities. Although the language they use tells us many things, preschool children often lack the ability to translate their wants and feelings into words. They depend on adults to figure out what they need, want, and mean through their actions. In addition, the group interactions of young children are complex, and the groups are larger than during the infancy/toddler age (which compounds the interaction possibilities).
- Adults who nurture **school-age children** must remember that personal and peer relationships are constantly changing. School-age children are moving from a sphere of adult influence to one where peer influence is paramount, yet they don't all do equally well at the same time.
- Adults who nurture children in **family child care** settings must be skilled observers because they often serve children in a wide age range. A multi-age setting increases the complexity and variety of children's interactions and expands the range of growth and development issues addressed within the group.

Each child is different, just as each age is different, so people who teach and work with young children must be good observers. Developing keen observation abilities is essential to our understanding of young children, and certainly determines our own effectiveness with them. Jimmy Hymes believes that "Behavior talks!" We, the adults who work with young children, must be prepared and equipped to listen skillfully to what their behavior is saying.

There are six chapters in this book. Each provides ideas that apply to all environments in which adults work with young children. Each chapter is designed to help you better understand the issues related to observation as well as acquire skills for applying that information in your work with young children.

Observation is the first and most authentic tool for assessing young children's learning and development. Good, objective observations are records of children's growth and development. They are just as important as charts of height and weight. Good, objective observation records document milestones in the development of a specific human being—an individual child.

The information you gather from objective observation can also make an important contribution to the evaluation and improvement of your overall program. Knowing what goes on for children is a good place to begin evaluating the experiences you provide for them. So, read on to build your observation skills.

-Chapter One-

Looking and Seeing Are Different: What Is Observation of Young Children All About?

    I Spy! Remember that game? You probably played it as a child. In the game I Spy! each player takes a turn choosing an object. The other players look around and try to figure out, by asking questions, what was chosen.

    The goal of good observation skills is similar. By tuning in to the specifics of young children's behaviors, we gain a better sense of what the child is all about. Thoughtful teachers often pose questions about a child's behavior. One source of answers can be found in direct observation of that child. Yet, these answers often raise new questions.

    Our senses help us tune in to the world around us. Sometimes we remember many things we notice, see, or hear. Just as often, though, we loose track of what we have seen or heard because we are constantly taking in new information. Many experiences don't seem important to us, or we don't see reasons to remember them.

Observation of young children's actions and behavior means carefully paying attention to the details of what each child does and to the cues the behavior tells us about how the child feels and thinks.

    Just as in the game *I Spy!*, details are important. Meaningful observation of children's actions is more than just looking at what the child does. When we pay attention to the subtleties in the child's behavior, mood, and language, we gather useful information, and meaningful observation occurs. Noting details of the child's actions is important. How the child stands or holds a paint brush can be major clues about the child's feelings, skills, or level of confidence or knowledge.

Children's words tell us many things. A child's use of language and vocabulary provide a sense of the child's language facility and breadth of experience. Pronunciations and expressions are clues to family background and life at home. Comfort with language, frequency of speech, as well as tone of voice and pitch, provide important windows on the child's identity and experience.

One word of caution: children sometimes use words and expressions they have learned by rote and which have little real meaning for them. Assuming that young children understand simply because they can use the words can be very misleading. Check for meaning by making careful note of the context of the language or by asking questions that will help you assess their understanding.

Objective Observation Means Suspending Your Value System

An Open Mind Helps You See the Real Child

Crash! Bang! Boom! A child pushes over a block structure. Most of us have a hard time watching this occur without making a value judgment about the action. An infant drops food from a high chair. To observers in some cultures, this action may appear to need adult reaction to correct it.

The block structure was destroyed. The infant has made a mess for someone to clean up. Adults often see and judge children's actions by behavior standards, which may vary among cultural or socioeconomic groups. Adult interpretations and reactions are usually based on personal values.

Objective observers see beyond our own value systems. We put judgments on hold (except, of course, if a child is in danger) in order to look carefully at children's actions. Objectivity is a must for useful observation data. If an action has been mentally labeled as *good* or *bad*, *acceptable* or *unacceptable*, we are likely to dismiss it from our thinking. After it is dismissed, it can no longer function to help us understand the child.

Labels become confirmations for our prejudicial view of the child or family. Value-laden labels reflect attitudes that muddy the waters of child-sensitive understanding. Labels get in the way of seeing what the action means to the child or what the action could tell us about her development. Labels lead to adult misperceptions because the child is seen through glasses tinted by the observer's personal biases.

Objective observers pay attention to a child's actions. Withholding judgment, however, permits us to maintain an open mind about what has happened. Thoughtful consideration—without snap judgments or jumping to conclusions—allows us to explore the meaning of the child's behavior. We are free to think about what the actions may imply about the child's thinking, feelings, capabilities, skills, or about who this child really is. An open mind helps us to see the real child.

The Visibility Trap and How to Avoid It

A trap which frequently ensnares beginning observers is the high visibility of some children and the relative invisibility of others. A child's level of visibility is related to a number of factors. Among these are: our personal values about the child's actions or behaviors, the amount and intensity of the behavior, each child's activity preference, the child's level of dependency on adults, and the child's social skills. Keeping adequate, organized records on *all* children means that the observer must get beyond personal preferences and purposefully focus on everyone in the group.

This first activity for you to do is one you may choose to repeat often. The data it generates will help you recognize the visibility level for individuals in a group.

Activity Time

Step 1. Without looking at the group of children in your care, write down all of their names. Try not to purposely list any one child or group (as all boys) first.

Step 2. Look at the list. Why did you list the first child first? What makes that child come to mind before all others? Think about your reasons and jot them down. Why is child number 2, second? Child 3, third? Look at the last two or three names on your list. Why did these children come to mind last?

(Note: If your group has only six children or fewer, look at the first name and last name you listed.)

Step 3. Save the list and your reasons. Repeat this activity on a regular basis, perhaps in a couple of weeks. Keep your lists and look for changes. If you are concerned with changes in the level of visibility for individual children, repeat this activity a number of times and chart the results. Do any of the changes correspond to children's growth cycles? For example, as two-year-olds increasingly challenge your authority, you may find the ones with the most intense need to be in control at the top of your list. Or, as three's become more eager to please, the ones that please you the most may end up at the top of your list. Reflecting on why children's names come to mind first may spotlight some important things about yourself and behaviors that you highly value in children.

Details! Details!
Your Mental Video Tape

    The more objective detail the observer notes, the more likely the observation will yield new insights about the child. Read the two descriptions of a child's behavior and answer the questions that follow.

A. Juan uses both hands to place two large hollow blocks side by side on the floor. He picks up a third hollow block and places it on top of the first block, visually checking to match the edges as he balances it. He continues to build for about 10 minutes, always using two hands to lift each block and carefully balancing each block on top so that he forms a rectangle with the blocks. The structure is three blocks high all the way around. He stands back and looks at the structure. He is smiling during the entire episode. He takes a step forward and begins to kick the structure. Each time he kicks he says "Boom! Boom! Boom! ..." The blocks fall into a tumble on the floor. His eyes open wide as he says in a loud voice, "Man, did ja see dat?"

B. Juan built a house with hollow blocks. He aggressively destroyed it, screaming as he did so.

Activity Time

1. Does description A or B give you the most complete picture of what Juan did? Think about why you answered the way you did.
2. What three specific behaviors (from the more complete of the two descriptions) do you think are necessary to understand what Juan was doing and feeling?
3. What one thing did you learn about Juan, or what Juan was trying to do, from the examples?

    The difference a detailed, objective observation can make in how you view a child's actions should be clear to you from this activity. Here is another pair of notes on a child's actions. Think about which sample provides more information on the child. Which is more objective?

A. Cherise is sitting in a high chair with three pieces of graham crackers on the tray. She reaches toward the left piece with her fingers outstretched. She closes her fingers around the piece, holding it between forefinger and thumb. She looks down at it, turns it over several times, and then brings it to her mouth, opening her mouth as she moves the cracker toward it. She chews on it briefly, leans over the side of the chair, and opens her mouth. The partially chewed cracker falls to the floor. Cherise watches as it falls, then moves her hand down toward the chewed cracker on the floor, opening her hand and extending all fingers toward the cracker. She giggles. She turns back around in the high chair and repeats the same sequence of actions with the other two pieces of cracker. After the last one has fallen, she turns back around and pats the tray a number of times. Turning back to look over the edge, she begins to whimper. "More!" she says.

B. Cherise starts to eat her graham crackers. She really likes graham crackers. She spits the soggy crackers on the floor, purposefully making a mess. She likes to make messes. When Cherise realizes she has done a dumb thing by throwing them all away, she cries for more.

Activity Time

1. Which of the examples of Cherise's behavior is influenced by the observer's value system and biases?
2. Think about the words or phrases in the samples that tell you about the observer's value system and biases. Can you identify at least three?
3. What is one thing you learned about Cherise, or about what Cherise was trying to do, from the examples?

Thoughtful, objective observers use eyes, ears, and brain to record a child's actions just as a video camera records actions. The observer's job is to make a mental video tape for later viewing and analyzing.

"To be or not to be..."
—a Part of the Action

Have you ever been aware that you were being observed by someone who was writing down what you said or did? Perhaps you felt nervous, self-conscious, or uncomfortable knowing the person was making notes about you. These are typical feelings. Did you change your behavior because you knew someone was watching? An observer's presence or actions may influence the person being observed to act in a different way. A true and accurate picture of the actions of others often requires unobtrusive observation.

For the many times when your are observing and must be unobtrusive, stay on the edge of the action instead of in the middle. Put some space between you and the child or children. Move to a part of the area where you can see and hear but where your presence will not interfere with events. Appearing to busy yourself doing something can be a helpful strategy. With experience, children become oblivious to being observed.

Spend a few minutes observing the children with whom you work. Try not to let your presence influence what they do or say. At the end of your observing time, write down two or three sentences about what you saw. If children were talking, what words did they use? How did observing without being part of the action feel to you?

"Tell me about ..." or Purposefully Asking for More Information

Most young children like to show their stuff without being asked. The frequent "Watch me!" command is a good example. But not all children ask for the attention. Sometimes, observers need to ask children to demonstrate an action or respond to a question. Young children often delight in performing for or talking with us, if we just ask.

In this case the observer isn't unobtrusive at all, but is an integral part of the action. Paying close attention to children and asking or commenting about what they are doing is a way to set the stage for your involvement, and it also lets children know they are important! By asking open-ended questions, you can learn a lot more about what children know and think, which is important as you plan activities.

On the other hand, taking over or directing what children do tells them they don't need to think!! Such action tells them the adults will do the thinking for them, and this is a damaging attitude for a child to establish. When adults take over, children cannot become the best they can be or learn to think on their own.

Activity Time

Here is an exercise with two parts. The purpose is to help you see the impact your presence can have on children's behavior. It will also give you a chance to practice observing.

Part 1. Talk or interact with a child when he is engaged in doing something he chose to do. Ask him to show you something specific about what he is doing. When you finish, write down what he did or said and how you responded. Focus on recording the sequence of the interchanges between you and the child. You should be able to get a sense of your impact on him in about three to five minutes.

Part 2. Now move to the sidelines or out of the immediate area. Watch what the child does with the object, material, or activity after you are no longer a part of the action.

1. Was the child more engaged with the object, material, or activity when you were a part of it, or when you were not?
2. How was your involvement different in the two situations? How would you describe the quality of the information you gathered in these two situations?
3. Identify factors in the two situations that seemed to make a difference to the child and his actions.

The circumstances of the observation will dictate whether the observer should be obvious to the child or not. Both conditions can provide meaningful information that will be useful in understanding a child and what she needs. The observer decides which of these conditions will best elicit the information needed from the observation.

Developing Observation Skills —Practice Makes Perfect!

The only way to become a skilled observer is through conscientious practice. Acquiring the ability to develop helpful observations is like any other skill—working at it enhances your proficiency and allows sharp observers to reap the benefits good observations bring. So, practice! Practice! Practice!

Chapter 4 introduces a variety of observation tools and strategies. Some tools will seem more user friendly than others. Each type of observation makes a contribution to understanding young children. Certain circumstances lend themselves to specific tools. After completing this chapter, you will be better prepared to choose the tool that seems easiest to use in any situation, and one that is likely to provide valuable information. Use various tools often so that they become like an old friend or as comfortable as your most wearable pair of shoes.

"Teacher, read it again!"*
—By Way of Review

Good observers share a number of characteristics. They note detail and maintain an open mind to what they see. At times good observers interact with children while observing and may need to ask questions to gather needed data. Because proficient observing requires skill, considerable practice enhances observation ability.

*Quote from film *Foundations of Reading and Writing*

-Chapter Two-

Figuring Out the Puzzle:
How Observation Pieces Fit Together

Developing meaningful observation records is a little like putting jigsaw puzzles together. Noting specific details is one strategy for success. The shape and color of the pieces and background, as well as patterns of lines and curves, are details that assist in completing the puzzle. With all the possibilities in mind, the puzzle solver reflects on where each piece seems to fit. Sometimes pieces look like they will be just right until careful examination shows that they don't fit at all. Often a piece needs to be tried in several places before locating its spot.

Looking at children is a similar process. The pieces of data gathered on children through observing are like the puzzle pieces. Solving the observation puzzle involves making meaning from many pieces of data and trying to arrive at a better understanding of the child. Unlike the jigsaw puzzle pieces, observation data often fits many places. Determining whether or not a placement is accurate may take time, reflection, and additional observation. Data—gathered from many observations and carefully analyzed—can help observers see patterns in children's behavior and development.

When the pieces from repeated observations are put together, a picture of a whole child in context begins to take shape. Making meaning of children's actions is a major purpose for putting the observation puzzle together.

"Mirror, mirror..." or Reflection
—It's What Goes on in Your Head

Written records provide an opportunity to think about observed behavior, to reflect and re-experience the child's action, and to ponder meanings for observed behaviors. *Reflecting* on recorded behavior is another strategy that enhances understanding of children's behavior. Reflecting is as important to understanding young children as recording their behavior. This second part of developing written observation records generally goes on *in your head*.

Talking with others who are knowledgeable about children will extend and expand your ideas. Confidential discussions with others can help clarify your thinking about the behavior. As you work to identify the pieces and see how they fit together, a picture of who the child is will begin to come into focus. Reflection on observed behaviors often results in hunches to test.

Each time a written observation is reread, forgotten details will come to mind. New insights about children emerge through engaging in the processes of rereading and rethinking observed behaviors. Putting an observation into words and sharing it with another teacher is another helpful strategy. The process of organizing your thinking into a cohesive statement that others can understand improves your understanding of what you observed.

Hypotheses or Inferences
—Hunches Versus Judgments

A scientist often begins trying to find a solution to a problem by forming a *hypothesis*— an idea about what might be causing something to occur, or, when observing children, a source for the child's actions. A hypothesis is an educated guess. After a hypothesis has been formed, the researcher gathers more data that will either support or not uphold (refute) the hypothesis. A hypothesis is not considered the answer until further research verifies that the hypothesis is accurate.

Like the scientist, conscientious observers use our informed opinions to form hypotheses about children's behavior from actions we observe. Continued observation and data gathering is essential before we reach conclusions about a child's development. We must guard against jumping to conclusions based on only one or two instances. As the picture comes into focus, our ideas become inferences, or more hypotheses about the child. Even so, these inferences or hypotheses may begin to influence our actions with the child.

Jumping to Conclusions
Is Like a Half-baked Cake

Just as a cake that is taken out of the oven too soon falls and can't be served, reaching a conclusion about a child based on a single first observation can't serve the child well. Jumping to conclusions with insufficient data is unfair, leads to invalid conclusions, and is often dead wrong. How much data is enough to reach a reliable conclusion? The guiding principle should be that **you probably have sufficient data when the behavior is observed often enough to decide it is typical for the child**—that the behavior represents a common pattern of behavior for the child.

Even though an idea about a child's behavior or development appears to be supported, be prepared for contradictory evidence. Contradictions may result from changes in her mood, environment, family events, or peer involvement. Changes may be evidence that she has new capabilities as the result of growth and learning. In any of these cases, the original conclusion is inaccurate.

A solid child development background is the framework for figuring out possible meanings of children's behaviors. If reflecting on or developing inferences about observed behaviors seems difficult, it could well be that your knowledge about child development may need strengthening. Making sense of children's behavior is always difficult, and without a thorough knowledge of child development, the task is nearly impossible. Without knowing how children grow and learn, inaccurate or incorrect conclusions are a real danger.

Ways to learn more about how children grow and learn
- Take courses in child development
- Study a comprehensive child development book
- Work closely with someone who knows about and understands children and their development. A mentor who is willing to support your learning will increase the benefits gained from improving your observation skills.

When early childhood educators KNOW MORE, we DO BETTER! The purpose for observing young children is so that we know more about each child and become better able to respond to each one as a unique person.

"You must remember this..."
—Write It Down!

      Memory overload is one very important reason for writing down our observations. The human brain only keeps so much information accessible and current. Much of what we experience is remembered only for a short time and then dismissed. With so many actions and behaviors from each child each day, it is impossible to remember everything we see without making a written record. Memory overload happens to all of us, so don't think it's your age! It's not!

      Writing things down causes us to think about the ideas that are part of the information. Documenting children's actions in an organized, written form gives us a record of children's growth and development, their strengths and limitations, their needs, their interests, and their wants. All this enables us to nurture children in ways that enable them to flourish.

A solid child development background is the framework for figuring out the possible meanings of children's actions.

Do you remember everything you need when you go shopping? Most of us do OK, but function much better with a written shopping list to ensure that some necessary item doesn't get overlooked. This same principle applies to remembering information and reflections about a child's behavior.

A written record of inferences and hypotheses is essential, too, so that we can refer to our notes in the future. When you 1) write down a series of observations that occur over time and 2) record your inferences about the child, then it is possible to 3) assess the child's growth and progress for that time period, and 4) make hypotheses about the behavior.

"Teacher, read it again!"
—By Way of Review

Let's review the parts of the process for developing a written observation record before moving on to explore some ideas and techniques for developing good written observation records.

Steps in making a well-developed observation record

Step 1. Observe and write. Pay careful attention and then write down what the child actually does or says.
Example: You just observed a child for about 10 minutes. After you finished observing, you wrote down as much objective information about his actions and language as you could remember.

Step 2. Think and reflect. Think about what has been observed and then reflect on those observations.
Example: Then you thought about what you saw, reflected on the child's actions, and wrote down your thoughts and reflections.

Step 3. Form hypotheses. Connect the reflections with what is already known about children and their development. Write down hunches about individual children. Form hypotheses in an effort to make sense of many observed behaviors.
Example: Perhaps you came to some inferences or hypotheses about who the child is or what his needs are. This summary step in developing

written observation records may take a series of written records for your ideas to be accurate and complete.

All three steps are essential for your understanding of the child. Any one by itself is interesting and perhaps of some help. However, for observing to really pay off in understanding children, you must spend some time on all three steps—observe and write, think and reflect, and form hypotheses.

-Chapter Three-

Significant actions and language worth recording can occur at any time or place.

How To's and Other Clues

In this chapter we'll look at some techniques to use when developing good written observation records. Beginning observers often ask "How do I start?" Begin by keeping your eyes and ears open for something interesting that a child is doing or saying. This happens all the time with young children. An interesting action sequence or event can occur as children arrive and are being greeted, as an adult helps a toddler toilet, or while watching a four year old run across the yard. Significant actions and language worth recording can occur at any time or place.

Good Observers Are Like Boy Scouts
—Always Prepared

Effective observers are always prepared. One never knows when an interesting event will occur. Keep something handy to write on and with. A shirt pocket or the top of a cabinet out of the reach of very young children can be an accessible storage spot. When observing children who are using crayons or pencils, use what they are using. When their teacher models writing, children want to write too. One of children's primary motivations is to be like the important adults in their lives.

Remember the Activity Time at the end of Chapter 1 where you interacted with a child and then moved away and watched? In that activity, you compared the child's actions and language in the two situations. As you begin to do written observation records and make decisions about where and when to observe, think about what happened during that activity.

Keep in mind that what you observe may be influenced by the presence of adults. Where you choose to observe should be based on your relationship with the child, her comfort with you, and on the observation's purpose. Many highly informative observations just happen when they are least expected.

Mission Impossible?
Truly Focused Observing

Developing the ability to zero in on what one child is doing may seem like *Mission Impossible*, especially for teachers. We have to keep a finger on the pulse of the group, an eye on all that goes on. Focusing on only one part of the whole picture doesn't seem natural or comfortable given the responsibility for providing supervision for the whole group. Yet, the ability to concentrate on one child is also a critical skill.

Focusing on one aspect makes it easier for you to note specific details. Having a purpose—and knowing why that purpose is important—will help you see meaningful behavior. A purpose will help activate your mental video camera to record child behavior and language.

Focus can mean

- centering on the behavior of only one child in a group
- looking for specific skills or behaviors whenever they occur
- attending to the indicators of development in only one area such as language or prosocial skills

There may be times when the purpose for an observation is to see how a child interacts with others. That makes looking at the whole situation important. When a number of children are interacting, it may be hard to focus on just one child. Perhaps seeing how he responds to others is your intention. Focusing on what he says, how it is said, and the actions that accompany the language may provide important clues.

A ctivity Time

1. Decide on an idea, skill, or capability related to physical development that you can observe in a child's actions or language. For what will you be looking?

Observe with the purpose of looking for this idea in a child's actions and/or language. Write down what you observed. Share what happened in your observation with someone who understands children.

2. Write down two inferences or hypotheses indicating what you learned about the child's physical development. Repeat this process for several other areas of development. Try focusing on areas such as cognitive development, sense of self, communication ability, self-control, social development.

Complete observations include recorded actions and language, the observer's reflections, and inferences or hypotheses about the meaning of the behaviors. Observers can't plan when significant clues will appear, but can be purposeful in their focus. BE PREPARED is the motto of the skilled observer.

Good Mechanics Need Proper Equipment (and Observers Do, Too)

Beginning observers often wonder about what to use to write their notes. Use whatever you have available that seems to meet your needs. Here are several suggestions with some of the advantages and limitations of each.

1. **Index cards**
   a. Index cards are a good choice for several reasons. The 3 x 5" size allows them to fit easily into pockets or on top of furniture. Filing them under a child's name in a file box with dividers makes them accessible.
   b. Observations on separate cards allows observations that are similar to be grouped together. This makes it easy to share notes on a single observation with families to let them know about the day's events—accomplishments, issues, needs—and then file it for future reference.
   c. A cross-reference system makes it easy to find observations with more than one child. Simply write "See _____ (first child's name) on _____(date)" on another card and file it in the second child's section. No rewriting is necessary.
   d. Cards placed in a file box also make it easy to quickly determine which children are highly visible and which ones are less visible. This provides helpful information about which children need conscious attention in order to have adequate data about their growth and development.

2. **Notebook**
   This is a good choice because it makes available all observation notes in a single place. Notebooks often work well for a sequential record of actions.

Although notebook pages can be tabbed to identify specific sections for each child, notes often are not as easily reorganized as they are on cards.

To avoid this problem, some observers use gummed labels (see #4). The notes can then be organized in a number of ways before they are stuck into a notebook or onto sheets of paper.

Notebooks make ensuring the privacy of families more difficult because observation notes on all children are readily available to anyone looking at the records.

3. Sticky notes (such as Post-it™ notes)

Sticky notes have most of the advantages of index cards. They are separate, can be organized in any order, and can be reorganized easily if needed. This separateness is desirable if daily observation notes are to be shared with families.

Using sticky pads makes it easy to sequence observation notes and add information gathered over time. Also, sticky pads can be placed around the room, making them handy when the opportunity for an observation comes along.

Because they are not as sturdy as index cards, sticky notes are not as easily stored. They also stick together or may be difficult to keep neatly arranged when their stickiness begins to wear off.

4. Gummed labels

Depending on their size, gummed labels may not provide enough writing space to adequately record significant behavior. On the other hand, limited space can be an asset, as labels force the writer to be concise. The advantages and limitations are similar to those of sticky pads. The biggest drawback is that after the label has been affixed to a piece of paper, generally it is there for good. This seems to limit your flexibility. However, if labels are readily available and suit your needs, use them.

We'll look at some suggestions for an organizational system for keeping up with observation notes later. Being able to look back, seeing similar behaviors and actions over time, makes it possible to identify patterns in growth and development as well as progress.

Activity Time

1. Think about the four suggestions for writing down observation notes— index cards, notebooks, sticky pads, or gummed labels. Consider the advantages and limitations of each type. Which do you prefer as a beginning observer? Why?
2. Choose a child for a two- or three-minute observation. Use your preferred type. Did it work as you thought it would?

"I'm late! I'm late!
No time to..." Observe

People who work with young children have many demands on our time and attention. Sometimes teachers feel there isn't time to observe and write about what children are doing. However, insights gained from purposefully seeing children's actions and language make observations a worthwhile time expenditure.

The secret to the time dilemma is to keep observation notes brief. Make them concise and precise. Use short, descriptive words. Get right to the action. A self-developed version of shorthand or abbreviations may also be helpful. Your notes are for *you!* If you plan to share them with families, you will want to write them so that the notes can be understood (or type them later).

When your notes are to the point and accurate, they will activate the detailed playback of your mental video tape. We remember more when we write down what we observe. The notes ensure that the right mental tape comes to mind for future viewing.

"It's a secret! I promised."
Observation Confidentiality

Finally, a word about the confidential nature of observation notes. All families want to be proud of their children. Few parents would want any of their child's developmental concerns to be broadcast to the wider world. Parents have the right to share information about their children with others or to choose not to share that information. Teachers are responsible for ensuring the confidentiality of all data on children in their care. Respect for family privacy is part of ethical teaching behavior.

Treat all observation notes as confidential. Respecting the privacy rights of families means that observation notes must be kept in a secure place. While this is important for records of actual behavior, it is even more critical when there are written inferences or hypotheses about the behavior. Observation records and summaries are like personnel records for adults. Access to them should be limited to the observer, the child's family, and other professionals who need to know in order to better meet the child's needs!

Behavior Talks!
But What Does It Say? Or Mean?

Actions speak louder than words. This adage is especially true for young children. Because of their newness in the ways of the world, they can't always say what they mean with words. A young child's natural inclination is to act—and his actions are our window to his world. When teachers don't observe and understand what we see, it is like looking through sheer curtains. We see images but without clarity. When teachers observe and understand, a child's actions take on new meanings. The window is clear, and we have an unobstructed view. Only then can we act in concert with the child and family.

We have all experienced childhood, albeit at a different time and under somewhat different circumstances. We know from our own experiences— as parents, teachers, or neighbors—some of the issues and needs of children. But the world of each child is one of many individual variations on the themes of development. Skillful teachers have to work to understand each child. Where to begin?

First, we need to know and understand what is typical for a given age,

A child's actions are our windows to her world.

and how typical development progresses. To recognize a meaningful behavior, one has to know the course and direction of human development. Child development research and theory—available in professional journals, books, videos, and classes—is a key resource. With a solid frame of reference of how children develop, teachers can begin to translate the language of child behavior. The more complete our understanding of typical development and the child's issues, the easier this translation becomes.

Another factor in determining meaning has to do with the intensity of the behavior. A child's actions that occur repeatedly and with great intensity are significant. Frequency and intensity are two major clues to the child's level of meaningfulness of an action. When frequency and intensity are characteristics of a child's behaviors, adults need to pay attention to the child. When these two characteristics are present, the child has made a major investment in communicating an idea to adults. We need to listen.

So what does a child's behavior say? What actions are meaningful? That depends on our knowledge of children, our frame of reference about children, and our ability to listen to the child through observation.

"Teacher, read it again!"
—By Way of Review

Let's finish this section with a list of characteristics of good observation records. Think back to what you have learned. Each characteristic should jog your memory.

Good observation records. . .

- Contain **objectively recorded** data (No interpretations of meaning!)
- Are **detailed**, include **specifics** of action (Remember the pairs of observations of Juan and Cherise on pages 14-15.)
- Tell **accurately** what occurred (Focus on the actual events and what was seen)
- Include **exact language** used by child (Clues to feelings, knowledge, confidence, and wants)
- **Concisely** and **precisely** present the action (A clear, efficient picture)
- **Protect the privacy** of the child and family (Confidentiality is always maintained)
- Focus on **meaningful events** (Those related to child's development)

Activity Time

Look back at any of your observations. Answer each of these questions.

1.	Is it objectively recorded?	yes	no
2.	Does it include specifics of child action?	yes	no
3.	Does it accurately tell what happened?	yes	no
4.	Does the child speak during the observation?	yes	no
	Is exactly what the child said written down?	yes	no
5.	Is the observation concisely written?	yes	no
	Is it precise in wording and ideas?	yes	no
6.	Have I protected the privacy of the child and family?	yes	no
7.	Does the observation focus on meaningful child actions?	yes	no

---

Good written observations provide a solid basis for knowing each child. The key words for good records are:

**OBJECTIVE, CONCISE, PRECISE,
PRIVATE, ACCURATE,
and MEANINGFUL!!**

-Chapter Four-

"Mary, Mary, quite contrary. How does your garden grow?"

Tools to Cultivate Observation Skills

We have already defined observation, looked at some important considerations for good observations, and considered some helpful techniques for tuning in to young children. Just as sandwich meat is usually placed between two slices of bread, the meat of observation skill building is in the middle of this book. In this chapter we look at several families of observation tools, each of which has similar characteristics.

Conversation or Interview Family
Checklist Family
    Checklists and Rating Scales
    Event Samples
Time Sample Family
    Spot Check
    Time Tally
    Formal Time-structured Time
      Samples
Anecdotal Record Family
    Behavior Diary or Running
      Log
    Behavior-unit Anecdotal
      Records
    Incident Records
    Narrative

Tools are arranged from the easiest to use to the most sophisticated and technical. The exception is that the **formal time/structured time sample** is more involved than many of the tools in the **anecdotal record** family.

You will learn to how to decide which tool will provide you with the information you need most. There are advantages and limitations for each tool, so no one tool fits all situations. The tools at the beginning of this chapter most likely will feel comfortable to you, but comfort isn't the only consideration when choosing an observation tool. The right tool for your purpose will enhance your ability to understand each child and assess her learning and developmental progress.

There are three parts to the discussion of each observation tool:

1. **What is it?**—A definition and description of each tool including the type of information you can expect to gather when using it
2. **What does it look like?**—An example of a written observation using each tool
3. **When should I use it?**—Suggested uses and the advantages and limitations of each tool

By the end of this chapter, you'll be able to compare the tools we've explored to make decisions about the most appropriate tool to use in a given situation. You, the observer, must choose the type that best fits your purpose and suits your needs.

Even before children have intelligible verbal language, we talk to them and get their responses back.

"Tell me about when ..." Conversation or Interview Family

1. What is a conversation or interview?

This observation tool is so simple. We all have conversations with children every day, probably many of them. If we really listen to what children say, we can learn a great deal about them. The purpose of this observation tool is to consciously remember and record what children say to us. You may not have thought of your conversations as an **interview**.

Even before children have intelligible verbal language, we talk to them and get their responses back. Our efforts to stimulate language development with infants are a form of conversation. Infants soon begin to apply the rules of conversation. This give and take, where we adjust our responses to the child, is the essence of the **conversation** or **interview** observation tool.

Interviews with young children look quite different from the structured, formal interviews often used with adults. As we all know from experience, young children do not do well with a long list of predetermined questions. Typically, their attention begins to wander by the second or third question. Rather than answer our questions, they are likely to steer the direction of the conversation with ideas of their own. Yet, a skilled observer, who takes cues from the children, will learn a great deal from talking with them and begin to better understand the individuals.

Many factors influence the degree of success an adult has with a **conversation** or **interview**. Consider these:

- the child's level of trust in the adult
- the child's mood or feelings during the conversation
- the nature of the child's current activities
- the child's overall language ability
- the child's familiarity with the topic
- the child's view of how relevant the questions are

Each factor will influence the depth of information you obtain about the child and help determine whether or not the conversation gives you the information you feel you need. Letting the child take the lead and remaining open to where she takes the conversation generally yields the richest results. Children will share many things. Some may surprise you. In fact, you may find out more than you really want to know about certain aspects of family life.

During a **conversation** or **interview** intended to be used to gather observation data, do your best to record the child's exact words. Use spelling approximations for articulation errors because you are gathering information about the child's language development. Some phrases or child-created words are highly significant and should be written down. They have the potential to provide insight into who the child is and how he is thinking or feeling. However, because conversations occur all the time when working with children, you may have to settle for recording a summary of what the child says. If you are always on the lookout for new and different or particularly interesting things a child says, you'll be more likely to get good information.

When using observation data for assessment, record language samples frequently. A **language sample** is a written record of the child's exact spoken words. The best language samples occur in the context of a child's activity, usually in conversations with you or with other children. To obtain a valid and accurate picture of a child's language progress, make a series of language samples taken over time. Be sure to date each sample. These can be compared to demonstrate the child's growth and progress.

2. What does a conversation or interview look like?

This brief **conversation** (Figure 1) occurred between a teacher assistant and a young four year old. Several children are gathering near the snack table. For this group, snack is handled independently by the children and at the time each child chooses during the one and one-half hour free choice time.

January 21, 1997—Jeff is standing near the snack table.

Teacher: "Jeff, please sign in today." Jeff walks to the snack table.

Jeff: "I got my name. John, John, John... John! John is this you?" Jeff picks up an egg with Sara written on it.

Teacher: "This one is John's. Why don't you ask him if you can put his egg in for him?" Jeff is about to place John's egg in the carton.

Jeff: "John, you wanna your egg in?" John answers no, he's not ready for snack yet.

Teacher: "Jeff, I really do need you to sign in. Come on, I'll help you," taking Jeff by the hand and walking to the sign-in table.

Teacher: "Is this one your name?" pointing to his name card.

Jeff: "Yeah."

Teacher: "Where is John's name? You put your name card next to his name."

Jeff: "Is that John?" pointing to John's name card located next to where Jeff has placed his name card. Jeff points to his own name card and says, "That's MY name!" with a big smile on his face.

Figure 1. Recorded conversation

This was a short interchange but several significant pieces of information are apparent about Jeff. Did you notice that. . . ?

1. Jeff recognizes his own name, but does not yet recognize John's without a prompt.

2. Jeff seems pleased with himself for reading his own name.

3. Jeff communicates meaning very well even though some of his words aren't in complete sentence form.

Here's another sample, an **interview** (Figure 2) Lily is three and one-half years old and is sitting alone at the art table when a teacher assistant joins her. Lily does not look up.

February 4, 1997—Lily is sitting alone. She has drawn several house-like figures on her paper.

Teacher: "Lily, what an interesting picture. Would you tell me about it?"

Lily: "Those are two houses with kittens." She does not look up and continues to draw squiggles on her paper.

Teacher: "Oh. I have a kitty at home. Do you?"

Lily: "Yes. I have three kitties."

Teacher: "Do your kitties have names? What do you call them?"

Lily: "Burger Bob...he's kind of mean." She giggles.

Teacher: "Why do you think he's mean?"

Lily: "Oh, because he is sooo fat." (said matter-of-factly)

Teacher: "I wonder why he is fat?"

Lily: "Because he eats a lot. Fatty, fatty, fatty...." (in a sing-song fashion)

Teacher: "What do you feed him to make him so fat?"

Lily: "My mommy feeds him salmon, and then her looks for a place to go pee." (Note the use of "him" initially and then "her" for the cat.)

Teacher: "Where does he go?"

Lily: "The next one is kind, he's skinny." Smiles.

Teacher: "Does he eat salmon, too?"

Lily: "He doesn't eat too much...."

Another teacher: "Lily would you like to have snack now?"

Lily: "So full now, I don't want to eat snack."

Teacher: "Why are you so full? Did you just eat breakfast? What did you eat?"

Lily: "Toast on jam, I mean cinnamon toast. My mommy made it for me."

There is a pause in the conversation.

Teacher: "Lily, tell me about what you just drew on your paper." (pointing to a letter "L" inside one of the houses)

Lily: "That is a L."

Teacher: "Does the L stand for Lily?"

Lily: "I can only write a L."

Figure 2. Sample of an interview

The conversation continues for several more minutes. *Figure 2* reflects a longer interchange and includes a number of significant pieces of information about Lily. Try to answer these questions:

1. What did you learn about Lily's home life from her comments?

2. What academic skills does she let us know she understands?

3. What can you tell about her level of language development?

4. What did you learn about Lily's ability to stay with an idea? To elaborate on the idea and organize details about it?

Did you notice the kinds of questions the teacher asked in this sample? Often she used what are called open-ended questions. **Open-ended questions** ask for a response that is more than a single word answer or a statement of fact. They provide the child with an opportunity to think about the ideas and organize them in her own way. This helps the teacher begin to see how she thinks, organizes, and expresses ideas.

Activity Time

Here is an activity you can do with a young infant. It will help you understand just how early the cultural rules of verbal interchange begin to appear in humans.

Part 1—Interact verbally with an infant. Make a mental note of his reaction to your voice. Answer these questions.

1. Did the infant respond to you by vocalizing or making sounds when you repeated your words to him?
2. Did he try to make eye contact with you when he heard your voice?
3. About how long were you able to hold his attention?
4. Did some of your words or vocalizations hold his attention longer?

Part 2—Engage a child in conversation. Try to find a time when you can be close to the child without interfering with her purpose in play. Make this a personal one-on-one time. Talk with the child about what she is doing. Think about what the child says and take your cues of what to say next from what she says. Write down some of the child's language.

1. What is one thing you learned about the child from this conversation?
2. Was she comfortable talking with you?
3. What actions or responses helped you know about this child's level of comfort in conversing with you?

Information discovered or confirmed about a child from a conversation should become part of the observation data bank for him. Treat your conversation notes as you would any other observation. If you keep your observation data on cards, sticky pads, or sheets of paper, record what is significant and file it in your observation file.

3. When should I use an interview or conversation?

The examples, combined with your Activity experience, should help you see many uses and advantages of the **interview** or **conversation** observation tool. Teachers who ask questions and carefully record children's responses learn specific things. The teachers in *Figures 1* and *2* learned that each child knows certain things because each used those ideas in the natural course of events. Both are examples of authentic assessment of certain skills.

Conversations, by their nature, are a rich source of information on children's language abilities and level of development. The amount of language they use provides insights into their thinking and cognitive functioning as well as insights about their feelings, wants, and ideas. The tone of voice, speed with which they speak, and the number of words they use, in addition to their specific word choices, all provide teachers with windows on each child's emotional state. In addition, the language forms children use help us understand something about their view of themselves and level of self-esteem.

As with most things in life, there are no unmixed blessings. Although children tell us many things about themselves through their language, we shouldn't believe all we hear. Sometimes what they want so badly to be real appears real to them. Case in point:

> Four-year-old Mark was sharing with a teacher assistant a wonderful conversation about the new baby at his house. He was very graphic about the crying, feeding, and dirty diapers. He had all the language to create very vivid images of the new baby brother, and how his mom cared for Rolf. The teaching assistant was relatively new to the program and had not met Mark's mom. When she did, she congratulated her on the arrival of the new baby.

> Mark's mom looked a bit shocked and politely asked where the teacher assistant heard about the baby. She laughed and shared that Mark wanted a baby brother very much but that there was no baby Rolf at home.

Exchanges with a child's family give valuable information.

The moral of this story: If you expect what a child tells you to always be the truth, think again. If you have any doubts, confirm information shared by a child before acting on it.

Another value of the **interview** or **conversation** tool is its potential for helping you relate to families and for gaining insights from your conversations. Exchanges with a child's family are frequently a source of rich and important information for building your understanding of the child. Add insights gained from talking with families to your observation file for the child, and confirm what they say by observing related actions in their child's activities.

The interview or conversation can also be a tool for helping you solve classroom problems. I once used a conversation with a child in my second grade class to try to understand why I was seeing major changes in his behavior. One Monday morning Jerome came in, sat down at his table, put his head down, and fell sound asleep. I was concerned but decided he must have had a busy weekend. When the behavior repeated itself on Tuesday, I became more concerned. This was not typical behavior for Jerome.

Here's what our conversation sounded like.

Teacher: "Jerome, you seem really tired. Are you feeling OK?"
Jerome: "Yeah, but I'm really sleepy."
Teacher: "What did you do that makes you so sleepy?"
Jerome: "I watched TV last night."
Teacher: "You did! What did you watch just before you went to bed?"
Jerome: "Johnny Carson. It was really cool. My daddy really liked that movie star that was on, you know, the one that sounds like Briget Boardo..."
Teacher: "Bridgitte Bardot?"
Jerome: "Yeah, that's the one."
Teacher: "Sounds like you stayed up really late and that's why you're so tired."
Jerome: "Maybe, but my daddy said it was all right as long as I was in bed by the time Mamma got home from work."

By checking out the TV listing in the newspaper, I confirmed that Bridgitte Bardot had been a guest on the Johnny Carson Show. A quick call to Jerome's mom about his new behavior and his report of TV viewing resulted in discovering that Mom had started a new job working the four to midnight shift. She said she would take care of the situation. The next morning, Jerome was his old rested and alert self. Sometimes just asking *THE* right questions provides critical information that helps us understand what is going on for a child. I've always wondered what Jerome's mom said to his dad!!

A conversation or interview with a young child is more like an informal dialog than a formal, structured interview. Your ability to gather significant information from this observation tool depends on your conversational skills as well as a number of related factors.

"Check it off!"
Checklist Family

1. What is a checklist?

Checklists are among the most common observation tools. Almost everyone has used a checklist. A shopping list, a variation on the checklist theme, focuses our attention on a specified group of items. Because of the list, we are reminded to look for those items.

Observation **checklists** have a similar function. The items focus your attention on the identified action or behaviors. By design, a checklist preprograms your mental video camera to pay attention to and record only the checklist's specific set of actions or behaviors.

When we shop, we often notice and buy items not on our list. A similar phenomenon occurs when we observe. We see actions or behaviors not on the checklist. However, using a checklist means selectively noting certain actions or behaviors and ignoring others, at least initially. This intentional focus means you may miss many actions that are also significant. Using a checklist represents a conscious trade-off for having a preorganized set of items in mind for observing. Incidental information not specified on the checklist that seems important should be recorded in some other way.

A checklist can be used any time or place. The likelihood of encountering the behaviors on the list is enhanced when you observe at a time or in a place where those behaviors are facilitated. For example, if the checklist focuses on gross motor skills, the playground or gym might be most appropriate. If the checklist focuses on specific academic skills such as print awareness, obviously books or other printed material must be available for a child to demonstrate the skill.

Checklists are here to stay. They represent an efficient and abbreviated way to gather specific information on a child's actions and behaviors. Because they are used for many purposes, checklists seem to be everywhere!

A checklist that is set up to rate quality of the items on it, such as the one with the numbers 1, 2, 3, 4, 5 in the example that follows, is called a **rating scale**. Rating scales can provide very helpful information on a child's progress, especially if a series is kept for each child. By comparing each example taken over time, teachers can identify a profile of development. Major growth periods as well as plateaus become obvious. Almost any **checklist** can be converted into a **rating scale** by simply changing the evaluative part of the checklist to include a numerical scale.

2. What might a checklist look like?

A **checklist** has at least two key parts. One identifies the actions, behaviors, or characteristics that are the focus. The second part identifies a way to indicate something about each of the items on the checklist. Often this is an indicator of presence or absence, frequency, or the quality attributed to each item.

Given these essential parts, there are many variations for including items and describing the quality of what is observed about each item. One way is to focus on the **presence** or **absence** of the item. A good example of this is the yes-or-no, or shows-the-skill-or-doesn't form of quality indicator. This type of indicator typically means that the items are viewed as important characteristics or actions either to have or to avoid.

Figure 3 is part of a checklist-type observation tool designed by a teacher to provide her with some specifics about a child's responses to emotionally charged social situations. She did not include all items, but rather a selected few that piqued her interest and that fit the child in question.

Name _____
Date _____

	Behavior exhibited	
Description of behavior	yes	no
1. Crying	❏	❏
2. Sulking	❏	❏
3. Talking it out	❏	❏
4. Acting out physically	❏	❏
5. Asks for help	❏	❏
6. Ignores or leaves	❏	❏

Figure 3. Checklist tool. Child's responses to emotionally charged situations

One way to vary the information would be to add a column to describe something about the child's behavior. Another way would be to set up the chart so that the observer is looking for the **frequency** with which the items are observed. Indicators such as "at every opportunity" or "every time/often/seldom/never" would change the chart to indicate a frequency judgment for each item (Figure 4).

Name _____
Date _____

	Frequency of behavior			
Description of behavior	every time	often observed	seldom observed	never observed
1. Crying	❏	❏	❏	❏
2. Sulking	❏	❏	❏	❏
3. Talking it out	❏	❏	❏	❏
4. Acting out physically	❏	❏	❏	❏
5. Asks for help	❏	❏	❏	❏
6. Ignores or leaves	❏	❏	❏	❏

Figure 4. **Frequency checklist**. Child's responses to emotionally charged situations

This same checklist could easily be turned into another variation of the checklist family, the **timed tally**. *Figure 5* is the same checklist with the necessary modifications. The chart would be completed by marking observed behaviors with a tally mark each time that particular behavior is observed. Be sure to identify the time period for the **timed tally** observation.

Time period: From _____ a.m./p.m.   To _____ a.m./p.m.

Name_____Date_____

Description of behavior	**Frequency**
1. Crying	_____
2. Sulking	_____
3. Talking it out	_____
4. Acting out physically	_____
5. Asks for help	_____
6. Ignores or leaves	_____

Figure 5. **Timed tally.** Child's responses to emotionally charged situations

A series of observations taken at different times of day, or at the same time of day for a week or other specified period of time, would help a teacher begin to objectively establish a pattern of behavior for a given child. Having this type of information can be a convincing tool to help communicate with a family. When the items are arranged in a **developmental sequence**, even more information is indicated about the child. Consider the same six items rearranged to indicate a developmental progression in responses to emotionally charged situations (Figure 6).

Name _____   Date _____

	Behavior exhibited	
Description of behavior	yes	no
1. Crying	❑	❑
2. Acting out physically	❑	❑
3. Sulking	❑	❑
4. Asks adult for help	❑	❑
5. Talking it out	❑	❑
6. Ignores or leaves	❑	❑

Figure 6. **Developmentally sequenced checklist.** Child's responses to emotionally charged situations

Although there may be some question about the appropriate developmental placement for item six, in this context it means that the child doesn't see the situation as one that requires a response. The child is secure enough to not need to respond to maintain her emotional comfort.

Another way to indicate the quality of response on a checklist is to use **numerical indicators**, such as with 1 indicating poor and 5 indicating excellent. This modification would give the chart a rating scale format. However, if numbers were used for the emotionally charged situations example, the checklist wouldn't make sense. Those items don't lend themselves to using a numerical scale. *Figure 7* looks at some beginning literacy competencies, and works well with numerical indicators. It is an example of a **rating scale**.

Indicators	1*	2	3	4	5
Name_____Date_____					
1. Concept of print	❏	❏	❏	❏	❏
2. Directionality	❏	❏	❏	❏	❏
3. Alphabetic principle	❏	❏	❏	❏	❏
4. Voice/print match	❏	❏	❏	❏	❏
5. Concept of book	❏	❏	❏	❏	❏
6. Phonemic awareness	❏	❏	❏	❏	❏

*1 means little understanding, 5 means excellent grasp of concepts

Figure 7. **Rating scale**. Beginning literacy concepts and understandings

Now that you've seen some samples of brief and specific checklists, let's think about where to find **checklists** to use with young children. The ones you've just looked at were created by a teacher to gather specific information about a child.

Use a checklist when you need to know if a child is developing typically for his age.

Most often, unless the checklist is to be used for comparative assessment, the best **checklists** are developed by observers. Because self-developed checklists are tailor-made to the situation and include only information that observers need, they are very helpful. Developing a **checklist** isn't difficult. What is critical is knowing what you need to know and understanding enough about children's typical behavior and development to work with integrity and accuracy.

Major milestones in development are good items for a checklist. Any area of development that has an identified sequence has great checklist potential. For example, take the development of a child's sense of self. A sequential listing of significant indicators or major milestones could be turned into a helpful **checklist**. Using it to observe a child would provide information related to his current level of development in that area. This information would help you determine what you need to consider as you nurture his growing sense of self.

Here are some possibilities for setting up a **checklist** that looks at the child's sense of self (Figures 8, 9, and 10). The item used as an example is one early and major milestone in the development of a child's sense of self. There are samples of all three types of checklists described: **presence/absence** of the behavior (Figure 8), **frequency** of the particular behavior (Figure 9), and a quality rating or **rating scale** (Figure 10).

*This sample uses the **presence** or **absence** dimension, which is often called an **even sample**.*

Name_____Date_____

List of items or actions	Behavior exhibited	
	yes	no
1. Milestone or characteristic (example: Does child respond with recognition to her own image in mirror?)	❑	❑

Figure 8. Child's developing sense of self

*This sample sets up the checklist to look for **frequency** and uses the same milestone. This format is sometimes called a **behavior tally**.*

Name_____Date_____

Description of behavior	Frequency of behavior			
	every time	often seen	seldom seen	never seen
1. Milestone or characteristic (example: Does child respond with recognition to his own image in mirror?)	❑	❑	❑	❑

Figure 9. Child's developing sense of self

This sample provides an opportunity to make a quality rating for each item. This variation is referred to as a **rating scale**.

Name_____Date_____

List of items or actions	1	2	3	4	5
1. Milestone or characteristic (example: Does child respond with recognition to her own image in mirror?)	❑	❑	❑	❑	❑

Note: An essential part of a number scale is a description of the meaning of each number. In this sample checklist, 1 means little or no response and 5 means full recognition of the reflection as self.

Figure 10. Child's developing sense of self

---

3. When should I use a checklist?

Checklists are useful when you have a predetermined focus that will provide the information you need. Questions about specific skills and capabilities, or a child's level of overall development, can be answered by using a focused, specific checklist. The critical element is the quality and accuracy of the arrangement of items on the checklist being used. If you are a new teacher, you will need to find a reliable source for information about what is typical. The bibliography at the end of this book includes a number of good resources.

If you are an experienced child watcher, your own experience may serve you well. When you think about all the children you have known of about this same age, what seem the most obvious indicators of development common to all those children? This should help you think about typical behaviors and provide a resource for developing your checklist.

If your checklist items are clear and provide behavioral descriptions, others should be able to recognize a given behavior as indicating the same thing you think it indicates. Engage other knowledgeable child watchers to look at your items. Ask for their feedback. If they can clearly identify what you mean and you all recognize the same behavior as evidence of a given skill or capacity, your checklist will be more accurate. When this happens, you will be able to gather convincing information.

What if you would rather start with someone else's checklist, or one that has been developed by an expert in child development? Many, many sources exist. In fact, hundreds of checklists are available. Some have been standardized by using them in many different settings. Most books on observation, many child development textbooks, and most curriculum models or programs (such as High/Scope), contain at least one checklist. The items on many are similar because the typical sequence for developing certain skills is common for all children in a cultural group.

Your purpose will help you choose a source. If you want to know about a child's social skill development, look for a checklist that provides information on those competencies. If cognitive development is the area, look for a checklist with items indicating intellectual progress.

Be careful here. A listing of academic *skills* or specific *knowledge* is not the same as a checklist that would provide insight into cognitive *development*. A cognitive development checklist helps you see how to help a child learn rather than what the child does and does not know. Many so-called cognitive checklists are really listings of content and specific knowledge such as colors, letter names, and shapes.

Choose wisely. Know what you want to know and select a checklist that matches your needs—it will provide the best return on the time you invest in observing. The bibliography in the back of this book lists some sources.

The essence of the *checklist* family is the preestablished nature of the items to be observed. Checklists can be used to document the presence or absence of characteristics, actions, or behaviors; the frequency of these; or the quality of the characteristic, action, or behavior. Checklists focus attention on a limited number of items and help teachers learn specific things about children.

Major milestones in development are good items for a checklist.

"One moment in time..."
Time Sample Family

The name of this observation tool describes the technique. A **time sample** is a sample of behavior recorded at intervals during a specific time period. Many variations on this theme are possible, from rigid adherence to a strict schedule in which you observe, then record, observe again, and record again, to a more relaxed time tally. With time-sample tools, the focus is on time periods rather than the flow of events or concerns about looking for specific actions.

When time is the determining criteria, the resulting observation provides an incomplete record of behavior, rather than a continuous picture of the child's actions. The flow of the child's behavior may be interrupted. This is especially true for the **time tally** and the **spot check** variations. When recording the **formal time-structured time sample**, the observer's mental video camera is activated only during identified timed intervals. During periods when details are not being recorded, the observer's mental video recorder is turned off. Any observation variation that is time based is part of the time sample family.

A time sample is a good tool to use when you suspect a child is having a problem or when the child's actions strike you as unusual. The information gathered from a time sample can help confirm your hunches *and* provide documentation to support your concerns. Objective time sample information may make an important difference as you approach a parent, principal, or child care director with a request for special services or considerations for the child.

"Petite Time Samples"
—Spot Check

1. What is a spot check?

Need an easy-to-do observation tool? The **spot check** may be just the thing. This time-based observation tool doesn't provide a high level of detail, but it can still provide helpful data. The **spot check** resembles its name, as the observer locates the identified child at specified intervals of time to check out what she is doing.

Several variations are possible. One of the most common is to locate the child at given intervals of time and make brief notes on where he is and what he is doing at the specified time. Time intervals can be a particular time period of one day (such as every 10 minutes for a two-hour period) or at a particular time over a longer period (at 10:30 every day for two weeks).

2. What does a spot check look like?

Typically a **spot check** observation uses a chart to help you organize the information and remember the time intervals. The example in *Figure 11* organizes the data gathering into 15-minute intervals.

Child's Name _____ Maurice _____ Date ____ March 12, 1997 ____

Time observed	Child's location	Actions observed
9:00	Blocks	Stacking hollow blocks, making a fort
9:15	Blocks	Putting animal models into barn
9:30	Blocks	Jumping a cow over the barnyard fence
9:45	Snack table	Pouring own juice, no spills. Counting out 5 crackers for snack
10:00	Snack table	Helping George count out his crackers
10:15	Easel	Painting rainbow with right hand
10:30	Computer	Loading a program into CD-ROM
10:45	Computer	Using mouse to click on parts of picture

Figure 11. Spot check for gathering information at regular intervals

This chart provided the teacher with a sense of Maurice's involvement with materials during a portion of his morning. Note the length of his attention span for the block area. We also get some sense of his fine motor abilities. With the addition of a column indicating names of other children involved with him, we could begin to get a sense of his playmate preferences and his sociability.

Activity time

Here are some guidelines to help you do a **spot check** observation.
1. Select a child to observe.
2. Decide on a time for you to begin. Times when children make activity choices such as free play time or outdoor play time are the best times for learning about children.
3. Prepare your record sheet similar to the sample. Make changes in the categories and time intervals to meet your need for information.
4. Keep a pencil and your record sheet with you for your identified time period.
5. Find the child. Write your responses to your items.
6. Continue with your typical classroom activities but keep track of the time.
7. In 15 minutes, (or whatever time interval) locate the child and record what you see.
8. Repeat steps 6 and 7 for the rest of your specified observation period.

Look over what you recorded and reflect on your notes. What can you tell about this child's play preferences? Social contacts? Keep these notes to think about at a later time.

You may choose to repeat the observation at a later date with the same child. Is there anything different in the two sets of data? Try another spot check, but this time choose a different child. What did you learn about this child?

3. When should I use a spot check?

Because it is a simple observation to do and very flexible in format, the spot check provides a good way to begin using time-based observations. The length of time between brief observations in spot checks—as well as the kind of information to gather and the total period for gathering data—are all decided by the observer. Make modifications so that the time sample tool works to record the needed information.

Using a spot check for the free choice period every day for a week yields interesting information on a child's variety, or lack of variety, of activity choices. One way to vary the spot check is to record what a child is doing and where at the same time each day. Your data may reveal patterns for children's activities and behaviors. This approach is very helpful for the teacher who notices, for example, that a child's self-control falls apart at the same time each day or after a given activity.

"Once in the morning, again at noon..." —Time Tally

1. What is a time tally observation?

Let's look at another variation on the timed observation theme. Rather than being a sample taken at intervals, the **time tally** combines elements of a checklist with a frequency count. The simplest time tally is just a count of the **frequency** for a particular behavior during a given period. Another variation of the time tally shows the **frequency** and **timing** of a specified type of behavior or action.

Using a time tally can help to confirm your inferences about a child. It is an especially useful tool when you suspect the presence of a problem, a disturbing trait or characteristic action, or the appearance of a new skill or capability.

2. What does a time tally observation look like?

In the following **time tally** a child care provider wanted to better understand the extent and frequency of Vladimir's behavior (Figure 12). She was concerned because after only two days with him in her care, she was beginning to form a perception of Vladimir as a highly aggressive child. He seemed constantly intense. She felt she would have a more realistic picture of his aggressive actions by keeping a frequency tally.

Child observed: _____ Vladimir _____
Date: _____ February 12, 1997 _____
Behavior to be noted: _____ Aggressive, hurtful-to-others actions _____
Arrival time and pertinent conditions: _____ 7:30 a.m.; unhappy, agitated _____
Departure time and pertinent conditions: _____ 5:15 p.m.; out-of-control _____
Total number of tallied actions: _____ 28 _____

LHHT   LHHT   LHHT   LHHT   LHHT | | |

Figure 12. Sample time tally observation (*frequency* only)

By this simple process of tallying a mark each time she saw an aggressive action, the family child care provider was able to see the frequency with which the behavior occurred. However, the frequency was little help in deciding what might be causing the behavior. She decided to observe Vladimir the next day, adding a record of the times at which his aggressive actions occurred (Figure 13). She felt she would have a more realistic picture of how frequent and pervasive Vladimir's aggressive actions were.

Child observed: _____ Vladimir _____
Date: _____ February 13, 1997 _____
Behavior to be noted: _____ Aggressive, hurtful-to-others actions _____
Arrival time and pertinent conditions: _____ 7:32 a.m.; unhappy, tense _____
Departure time and pertinent conditions: _____ 5:12 p.m.; out-of-control _____
Total number of tallied actions: _____ 27 _____

Times when aggressive, hurtful-to-others actions were observed:

7:32	7:33	7:34	7:36	7:39	7:44
7:51	8:00	8:10	8:30	8:55	9:45
11:40	12:55				
4:15	4:35	4:50	4:56	5:00	5:05
5:08	5:10	5:11	5:11	5:12	5:12
5:12					

Figure 13. Sample time tally observation (*time of occurrence* recorded)

The teacher looked at the times and noticed that they occurred in clusters. The data made her wonder about what else was happening at these times. Vladimir's aggressive actions were most frequent at arrival and departure. He seemed to calm down after he had been in the group for a while. The aggressive, hurtful actions intensified as the end of the day approached. The teacher decided to modify the tally approach a third time to include some of the context in which she saw his aggressive actions occur (Figure 14).

Child observed: _____ Vladimir _____
Date: _____ February 14, 1997 _____
Behavior to be noted: ___ Aggressive, hurtful-to-others actions ___
Arrival time and pertinent conditions: ___ 7:36 a.m.; unhappy, tense ___
Departure time and pertinent conditions: ___ 5:10 p.m.; angry, out-of-control ___
Total number of tallied actions: __ 24 __

Timing for specified actions:
7:37	Punches Peppe who is already present
7:38	Pinches Rudolfo as Rudolfo arrives
7:40	Trips Maia as she arrives
7:43	Pulls chair out from under Maia
7:47	Takes book from Sam
7:52	Elbows Leif
8:00	Takes Mona's doll from her and throws it across room
8:12	Calls Rudolfo a name
8:30	Sits down on top of Anna
9:00	Takes Mona's book from her
10:10	Flicks forefinger and thumb at Sam 2 inches from nose
11:45	Tells assistant he hates her
1:00	Throws self on cot
4:20	Tells assistant she's mean and he hates her
4:40	Pushes Peppe down
4:50	Kicks sand at a group of children
4:58	Rides a trike into a tree with great force
5:04	Runs and crashes into Leif
5:06	Swinging arms around and hits Anna
5:08	Chases Sam and tackles him to the ground, punching him once, has him down on ground
5:09	Swings coat around with great force and hits two children
5:10	Pounds on older brother's legs (has come to pick up V.)
5:10	Kicks several times at Sam who is also leaving, connecting once

Figure 14. Variation on the **time tally** observation (with *specifics noted*)

By comparing the tallies for these two days, the teacher confirmed that Vladimir's most frequent and most hurtful actions did indeed happen at arrival and departure times. His hurtful behavior tapered off within an hour of arrival and began to increase in frequency and intensity as time to go home came closer. It occurred to her that at about the same time each day (around 4:15) Rudolfo's mother comes to pick him up. He is usually the first child to leave each day. Could Rudolfo's leaving be triggering Vladimir's aggressive action?

On the fourth day of observing, Rudolfo was absent. Vladimir's tally looked like this (Figure 15).

Child observed: __Vladimir__
Date: __February 17, 1997__
Behavior to be noted: __Aggressive, hurtful-to-others actions__
Arrival time and pertinent conditions: __7:35 a.m.; unhappy, tense__
Departure time and pertinent conditions: __5:10 p.m.; upset but calmer__
Total number of tallied actions: __19__

7:35*	7:36*	7:39*	7:45*	7:59	8:14*
8:32	8:55	9:20			
11:41	1:00				
4:55*	5:05*	5:07	5:08*	5:08	5:09*
5:10*	5:10*				

* times when a child arrived or departed

Comments: The first child to leave left at 4:55. That was the first tallied incidence of aggressive behavior since 1:00 for Vladimir. The 9:20, 11:40, and 1:00 times were fairly common times in all three tallies. These coincide with significant changes in activities for the children and are times when other children are less calm and settled.

Figure 15. Second sample **time tally** observation

The data on these four **time tally** observations (Figures 12, 13, 14, and 15) presents an interesting picture that comes into sharper focus with each variation of the **time tally**. Vladimir's teacher began to believe that changes in activities, and arrivals and departures, had something to do with Vladimir's pattern of aggressive actions.

3. When should I use a time tally?

The information from these four observations proved very useful to the teacher because she now had an established pattern of Valdimir's stressful times. She could anticipate them and provide extra supervision and assistance when activities changed. She could focus on providing help during transitions, especially those from home to child care and child care to home.

Her observations helped her become more objective about Vladimir's behavior. She was able to support Vladimir in changing his behavior, and alter the way the children were beginning to see him. The observations also provided helpful data to share with his family. In conference with his mother, the teacher learned that conditions at home just before Vladimir came to school were not always calm and nurturing. Knowing this helped the teacher understand even more about Vladimir's behavior.

Using a **time tally** technique, this teacher was able to see patterns in Vladimir's behavior and begin to try to assess how to help him. She now had more than her initial impression to help her make appropriate teaching decisions.

Activity Time

Doing a **time tally** observation

1. Select a child and characteristic action about which you would like to know more.
2. Record the time(s) when you observe the selected action during a given day.
3. See if there are patterns or clusters of times when the action is most frequent.
4. Repeat the time tally if you feel a second day's information would give you a better understanding of what you saw. By keeping a tally for several days, you may be able to identify factors that contribute to the action. You may decide to change the conditions, or you may want to see if the behavior occurs more or less often, given your new view of this action.

A **time tally** could just as easily be used to identify events such as the timing or frequency of an infant's irritability or sleep schedule or a toddler's attempts to master walking, speech, or other developmental milestones. The time tally is a highly versatile tool. After you master it, you will find many ways to use a time tally in your observations. The time tally takes very little time away from interacting with young children, yet it provides valuable and meaningful information about them.

The key element in the Time Tally is knowing what you want to observe and tally. You can enhance the versatility of the Time Tally by varying your records, such as noting the time these elements occur or noting some circumstances accompanying the behavior.

Focus attention on a single child and her actions, rather than looking at group interactions.

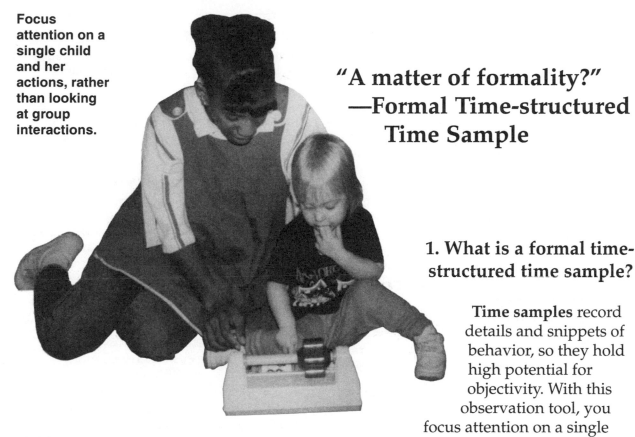

"A matter of formality?" —Formal Time-structured Time Sample

1. What is a formal time-structured time sample?

Time samples record details and snippets of behavior, so they hold high potential for objectivity. With this observation tool, you focus attention on a single child and her actions, rather than looking at group interactions.

Usually a 10-minute period of time is enough time to record a useful sample. Even more helpful is taking two 10-minute samples separated by at least 20 minutes. Most young children have changed activities by then, and the second sample provides information for comparing the child's actions on the same day.

A complete and useful time sample requires an investment of time and effort. You must engage in disciplined observation, pay careful attention to the details of the child's actions, and objectively record those details. The comments section is where you write interpretations after reflecting on and analyzing the child's actions. This is the place to practice all those ideas you learned earlier in this book.

2. What does a formal time-structured time sample look like?

Figure 16 shows a formal, structured time sample observation. The observer recorded it using an observe-for-one-minute/write-for-one-minute sequence, and then repeated the sequence four times. She took about a 45-minute break and then repeated the same observe-then-write sequence until she had five additional entries.

Clearly, the action is not continuous because the observer focused her attention on recording what she saw (not on the child) during the second minute of each two-minute entry. Each set of five entries also includes a brief introduction and some background information about the child.

Name_____   Date_____

Maria (age 4) walked into preschool clutching her blanket and sucking her thumb. When this observation begins, she has been standing just inside the door for 20 minutes. There were no tears when her aunt dropped her off at 8:45 a.m.

<u>Actions</u>	<u>Comments</u>
9:05 M. has her left thumb in her mouth. Her right hand is holding the blanket against her right ear. She slowly walks over to a table with a puzzle on it. M. stands next to the table, looking down.	M. entered slowly this morning. Her thumb and blanket seem to comfort her. She does not appear interested in the puzzle.
9:07 M. stands in the same position the entire minute. She rubs her eyes with her left hand then returns her thumb to her mouth. The blanket is still held against her ear.	M. seems tired. I think she may want to get involved but doesn't do anything. This reluctance is not M.'s usual pattern of action.
9:09 Berta walks up to M. and says "Hi." M. turns and looks at B. She doesn't say anything. She pauses about 30 seconds, takes her thumb out of her mouth, and rubs her eyes. M. sits down at the table with the blanket against her left ear.	This is M.'s first contact with another child this morning. B. and M. seem to be special friends and often play together. B. was late this morning and has just arrived.
9:11 M. is sitting in a chair at the puzzle table. Her left thumb is in her mouth. She holds the blanket against her right ear with her right elbow propped on the table. B., seated next to M., is putting pieces into a puzzle. M. stares at B.'s hands.	M. seems to watch B.'s actions but doesn't do or say anything. M. has held the blanket against her ear for 6 minutes now. Her overall muscle tension seems very low. She seems to take a passive, casual observer role.
9:13 B. says "Want to help me? It's fun." M. reaches for the puzzle piece next to her with her left hand. She slides it towards B. M. says, "Here."	Even though B. has tried to engage M. in conversation, moving the puzzle piece is M.'s first direct response to her friend. Perhaps she is left handed?

Maria and Berta are in the book corner. B. is sharing a book with M. B. holds the book, reading the story, and turning the pages. The girls have been together the whole time between observation parts.

10:00 M. sits propped against the wall next to B. Her left thumb is in her mouth and her right hand is holding the blanket up to her ear. She sits motionless with eyes fixed on the book.	B. seems very important to M., especially today. B. is the active one today, which is a bit unusual. Typically, they share equal roles in interaction, with neither one playing a dominant role.
10:02 M. rubs her eyes with her left hand. She picks at her ear under the blanket. She frowns. Her left thumb goes back in her mouth. She rubs her right ear with the blanket. M.'s eyes have a glassy look.	Here are more cues that something is not right for M. today. Looking back on this, it seems pretty obvious that she is either tired or not feeling well. Could she be bothered by an earache?
10:04 M. leans over and rests her right ear on the blanket, which is on the floor. Her cheeks are pinker than they were 4 minutes ago. Her eyes are only half open. B. continues to read to M. M. gently rubs her right ear.	M. appears almost asleep. Her flushed cheeks tell me I should check her for fever. She doesn't seem her usual active self today.
10:06 M. is still leaned over, resting right ear on her blanket and on the floor. She whimpers a time or two. B. stops reading and asks "What's wrong baby?" M. says, "My ear hurts." M. pats her on the head.	M.'s actions tell me that she's more than just tired. Her comment confirms that her ear is part of the problem. B. is M.'s very special friend and M. seems to appreciate the sympathy & comfort.
10:13 M. lays on her right side on her mat faced away from the door. Her eyes are closed and she is sucking slowly on her thumb.	M. seems comforted. Perhaps being in a quiet place on her mat makes her more comfortable. I'll keep check on her and call her mom if she doesn't feel better by lunch time.

End note: There is a break here because I stopped to tend to Maria. She asked to have her mat put down and has been resting on it for several minutes. She says her mom gave her some medicine for her ear this morning. Although she looked flushed, she did not feel warm to the touch.

Figure 16. **Formal, structured time sample** observation

Quite by accident, the teacher observed Maria when the child was not feeling well. Although she probably would have recognized Maria's needs without doing a formal observation, the cues during the observation made clear what was causing Maria's unusual response. Maria was very quiet about sharing her discomfort with an earache, even with her good friend.

Although it took a while, the teacher recognized that Maria wasn't feeling well. Going back to the time sample, the teacher began to suspect something was amiss in the 9:07 entry. Note her comment "not M.'s usual pattern." Prior to this entry, the teacher might have attributed M.'s behavior to Berta's late arrival or to being a bit tired. By 10:02 it is clear that the teacher recognizes that something is wrong. She continues to watch for cues in Maria's behavior and at 10:06, Maria's comment confirms her suspicions. Knowing that Maria's mom treated her earache at home may have led the teacher to make Maria as comfortable as she can and not call her mom immediately.

Perhaps you're thinking that is a lot of writing to figure out that a child has an earache. Indeed, it is. However, when the teacher began observing Maria, she didn't know that Maria was feeling ill. It was the careful observation that helped her know this. The comments in this observation are the teacher's reflections and notes from puzzling about the meaning of Maria's behaviors. (She wrote the comments during rest time, and not during the observation period, although some of the comments came to her as she observed.)

This teacher has developed her own abbreviated way of writing during observation periods. She comes back to her notes, usually during rest time, and fills in the words and any additional details she is sure she observed. Then she begins to reflect and write her comments.

3. When should I use a formal time-structured time sample?

The discipline necessary to write a **formal time sample** helps build skills of paying attention to detail. Watching carefully, and not writing, allows you to place full attention on a child's behavior.

Activity Time

Carefully reread *Figure 16*, the formal time-structured time sample observation, again. Answer these questions for yourself.

1. Was the recorded behavior complete enough to document something about Maria?
2. Was it objectively recorded without teacher bias?
3. Did you notice that the comments are the teacher's inferences and ideas about what she observed?

4. Did you recognize that recording Maria's language was an important clue for the teacher to make meaning out of Maria's behavior?

5. Even though this observation is about Maria, what did you learn about Berta at the same time?

In order to do this observation, the teacher had the luxury of removing herself from interaction with the children so she could give her undivided attention to observing. Lucky her! Not all teachers are that fortunate. However, even if you are the only adult with a group, you can still do a type of time sample. In the next section we'll look at several time sample modifications.

However, *IF* you do have a way to do a **formal time-structured time sample**, try it. Your observation skills will improve from taking the time to focus and write about details of a child's behavior as well as from writing your reflections about what you observed. The content of what you observe isn't the point of practicing. Developing observation skills is the goal. Here are some suggestions to help you get started.

Activity Time

1. For the first part of the **formal time-structured time sample:**

Select a child to observe closely. Set aside 10 minutes to do so. Make notes on the setting and any significant events or circumstances (such as new snow, birthday celebrations, dad out-of-town). Note the time you begin observing. Observe for about one minute. Then STOP observing and write brief notes for about a minute. Repeat the observing/writing sequence five times. With this sequence you alternate paying close attention to the child with recording her actions.

Remember, you'll only write about the five minutes you observe. What you record is only part of what happened, not an account of every action. Actions during your writing time are not part of the observation notes. Comments come later when you have a chance to reflect on what you saw. Stop formally observing and work with the children for about a half hour.

2. Second part of the **formal time-structured time sample:**

Look for the child you observed for the first part of the time sample. Make notes on changes in the setting, significant events, or circumstances. Note the time you begin observing. Repeat the observe/ write sequence again five times. Remember to alternate paying close attention to the child *and* writing down what you saw. When you finish, you will have five entries for this 10-minute time period just as you have for the previous 10-minute period.

At some later point, perhaps rest time, look over both sets of notes. Reflect on what you observed. Write down your comments, what you think your notes tell you about the child. Thinking about what you saw and writing about your thoughts will help you remember more about the child's actions and think more clearly about the meaning of these actions. If you are puzzled by what you observed, seek out someone with more knowledge and experience with children to help you.

The formal time-structured time sample— a record of what the observer sees—is the most time-consuming and, in many ways, the most complex of the observation tools. Yet, it has the potential to provide very specific data which can be invaluable to teachers. There is no substitute for the effect the formal time-structured time sample has on the development of keen, focused observation skills. More than any other tool, this one stretches the observer to note detail and remain objective.

Focus on the Whole Episode
Anecdotal Records Family

The fourth and final group of observation tools we look at is known as **anecdotal records**. Observations in the anecdotal family are characterized by episodes of behavior. The amount of detail depends on the observer's focus or purpose.

With any type of anecdotal records, your mental video recorder is running during the entire episode. Anecdotal records describe a continuous sequence of related behaviors. They provide a picture with a flow of the action. Anecdotal notes should appear as a sequence of related behaviors or an episode of behavior. Typically, the observer sees the actions in context and tries to include some data on all participants.

This family of observation tools provides information which is especially helpful for understanding children's social interchanges and problem-solving strategies. Because the young child's nature is to be active, recorded episodes typically include a child or children interacting with learning materials or people.

"Dear diary, today..."
—Behavior Diary or Running Log

1. What is a behavior diary or running log?

This observation tool provides an informal way to record significant occurrences and is one of the simplest and least complicated observation tools to use. Many teachers keep a diary just so they can remember classroom events of the year. The style is flexible and open, and is highly adaptable to meet your needs. The main characteristic of a **behavior diary** is the sequential arrangement of behavior, usually in chronological order as it occurred.

2. What does a behavior diary or running log look like?

The **running log** in *Figure 17* is part of one kept by a child care provider in a family child care home. Notice that the entries are brief and upbeat. Because of the nature of family child care and the fact that the care giver is often busy with other children when families arrive for pick up, this teacher chose to make her running log available for families to read. Her log focuses on the events of the day, not actions of individual children. Enhancing communications with families is another potentially useful application for this observation tool.

12/20	A rare, sunny December day! We stayed outside for almost two hours. We enjoyed making long shadows.
12/21	Everybody wanted to hear Bart's book about animals in winter. We looked for squirrels' nests in the trees. We think we saw one in the big maple tree out front of the house.
12/22	Today we made red and green dough clay. The children loved making it and cutting shapes out with cookie cutters. I have the recipe if you want a copy. We also enjoyed watching the snow come down.
12/23	Our special winter treats were a big hit! The children really enjoyed making the snow pudding with whipped topping mix. Be sure to use fresh snow if you do this at home.
12/27	I think the children missed each other over the holidays. They had such a good day together.
12/28	Snow again! We had a great time making snow figures and adding food coloring to cups of snow to see what happened.
12/29	Mrs. Ross, my mail carrier, stopped to drop off a package and we invited her in for snack. The children enjoyed seeing her uniform and asking her questions about what happens to letters. Maybe we should go see her at the post office.
12/30	The rain seemed to dampen everybody's spirits. We had more misunderstanding and tears today than we've had in a long time. Maybe holiday stress is catching up with us?

Figure 17. **Running log** recorded in a family child care home

---

This family child care provider used the **running log** to help the families picture their children's day. She wrote enough information so that families could talk about the events of the day. Her brief but helpful entries were written during nap time. Because they were short, she only needed to spend a few minutes writing. Using the log to share general information gave her the chance to share other more personal things about each child with families at pickup time.

The daily running log also substituted for a weekly newsletter. With only six children in her care and no easy way to do a newsletter, the log was a good alternative. The log was placed on a counter right inside the door where families picked up their children. She had them initial each entry when children arrived and departed, so it also served as her daily record for attendance. Because she didn't have a formal plan book, the running log also helped her remember what activities she had planned and when the children had done them.

Activity Time

Keep a running log for one week. Try the approach used by the family child care provider in *Figure 17*. Make your running log available for families to read. Ask them at the end of the week if they would like you to continue making a log available for them.

3. When should I use a behavior diary or running log?

Behavior diaries can be very subjective. Frequently the entries include personal feelings about the behavior, just as a personal diary often does. One excellent application for the **behavior diary** or **running log** is to use it for your own professional development or enlightenment. Write down your thoughts and feelings about what happens each day. This approach may help you gain insights into your own feelings, needs, triumphs, or frustrations.

If children are included in the entries, you will also have a way to explore your feelings and insights about them. However, if you plan to use the **behavior diary** or **running log** for observation of children and to keep a record of their actions, you will need to bring more objectivity to what you write about them. A professionally trained person refrains from focusing on his own personal perspectives when writing about young children's progress.

The chronological organization of the diary or log makes it less useful than some types of observation tools if the purpose is to record information on a specific child. Because of the order of information, all the entries must be reread to organize relevant information for a child. If there are several entries, this can take considerable time.

One alternative is to keep a log for each child. If you have a small group, this should work fine. However, if your group is large, this would be time consuming and cumbersome. Perhaps a better alternative is to use **incident cards**. This variation of a simple **behavior diary** can be constructed by using a series of incident records arranged by date. We look at incident records as an observation tool a little later in this section.

Behavior-unit Anecdotal Record
—Workhorse of the Family

We will deviate from the general pattern of looking at the easiest observation tools in each family before the more complicated. The **behavior-unit anecdotal record** needs to come before the incident records and narrative for comparison purposes.

1. What is a behavior-unit anecdotal record?

The **behavior-unit anecdotal** record focuses observer attention on anecdotes or action episodes. An episode describes a sense of unity and completeness of action. Complete anecdotal records include or at least imply:

- a beginning—something that stimulates what comes next
- a body—the main episode or occurring action
- an ending—something that brings the action to a close

A behavior-unit anecdotal record tells the story of the event with enough detail for the meaning of the episode to become clear to the observer.

Recording actual child language is an important part of anecdotal records. Young children's language often defines what the shared events will be in their interactions. Language is essential for children to establish and sustain their play. Without a record of the exact words each child uses, the significance of the play may not be apparent.

Sometimes, children use a great deal of language and speak so quickly that recording all of it is difficult. When this happens, your general sense of what was said is better than nothing. However, a truly complete picture needs a record of each child's exact words and approximate spelling of the pronunciation. Accurate assessments of children's language progress makes this a must.

2. What does a behavior-unit anecdotal record look like?

A **behavior-unit anecdotal record** makes note of an episode from start to finish. Usually there is an event which sets the episode in action, some related actions, and something that marks the end of the incident. Often one episode in children's play precipitates another, and that's what makes it difficult to determine the ending point. Think about it this way: *The episode is over when the behavior unit stands alone.* If you can stop recording and still see how children resolved the problem or met their self-established goals, you are at the end of the episode.

Interesting and informative episodes often unfold before our eyes. We can't always anticipate when a child's actions will tell us significant things. The best strategy is to follow that Boy Scout motto "Be prepared!" Watch and listen. You may decide partway through an episode that it provides significant information about a child, information you want to be able to remember. Begin writing down what you see at any point. Then go back and reconstruct earlier parts of the incident if you are not sure what happened before you began formally making notes.

The sample anecdote in *Figure 18* helped the observer learn some new things about both Warney's cognitive skills and his fine motor skills. The episode occurred during lunch time at a licensed center serving 50 children ages six weeks through five years of age.

Introduction: Warney (a young 4) is sitting at a lunch table with 5 other children. He has been eating for about 15 minutes. Most of the children have finished their taco salad and corn. A teacher walks over to the table and begins to put a spoonful of fruit cocktail on each child's plate. The fruit cocktail consists of green grapes and pieces of white pears and yellow peaches.

Observed Actions

Warney holds a fork in his left hand with a fist-type grip. When the teacher asks if he would like fruit, he says "Yeeesss! I weally, weally like fwu-it." She puts a spoonful of fruit cocktail on his plate. He looks at it for a minute and says "Yummie, fwapes and pawas and yewoes."

He scoots his fork under a grape. The grape moves across his plate but is not on the fork. He moves the forefinger of his right hand in to keep the grape from moving and pushes the fork under it. He lifts the fork, puts the grape in his mouth, and chews it with mouth partly open. He smiles and says "Fwapes." Warney repeats his actions eating all but the last grape. He says, "Fwapes is wound," as he stabs the last one with the tines of the fork and puts it in his mouth. After chewing it up he says, "That's all the fwapes. Now I eat the pawas." He uses the same scooting-under action to pick up pieces of pears. Now and then he uses his right hand to keep them from sliding over the edge of the plate. Sometimes he uses his right forefinger to pick out pieces of peaches that are mixed in with the pears. As he is finishing the pears he says, "Pawas are white squawes and these are yewoe squawes."

The observer says the yellow squares are called peaches.

Warney says "Ya, peaches, yewoe peaches." After about three bites using the same approach as for the pears, Warney says "I likc pawas bestest. They're the goodest." Warney continues eating until all the fruit is gone. He puts down his fork and turns around in his chair. He calls to Toni (the teacher), "Toni, Toni. Wook. I eat awa my fwu-it." She responds positively to him and tells him he can scrape his plate. He stands up and picks up his plate and cup and walks to the bucket.

Figure 18. Sample **behavior-unit anecdotal record**

---

1. Identify some significant occurrences in Warney's speech (Figure 18). (If the observer had not recorded the language with an effort to spell words like they were said, would you have been able to talk about those ideas?)

2. Identify some of the ideas Warney seems to understand or at least knows something about.

         Did you identify the colors that he already knows and names?
         Did you identify the shapes he recognizes and names?

3. What do you know about his thinking?

         Did you recognize that he was comparing the shape and colors of the pieces of fruit?

         The separating he was doing into groups based on some perceivable characteristic is called sorting. It represents one of the clues to Warney's cognitive development found in the episode. This action tells us that he is beginning to reason that things in his world can be grouped or classified. He also tells us that he recognizes that observable characteristics are one reason for putting things in groups. This is typical behavior for children of his age.

Asking families about activities they enjoy together provides valuable information about their child.

Activity Time

         Choose a child and do a behavior-unit anecdotal record. Remember to record what the child did and said in an objective way. What new insights did you gain from observing the child? Did you have trouble deciding when to begin and end the record? Remember to think about the three parts of a behavior-unit anecdotal record.

3. When should I use a behavior-unit anecdotal record?

Behavior-unit anecdotal records are extremely helpful when the purpose for observing is to gather information on a child in any area of development. Clearly, the recorded details in the observation of Warney were necessary for the observer to recognize and understand what was meaningful about his behavior. Knowing that he names some colors, identifies some shapes, and engages in some sorting activity—and recognizing that these are all significant actions—will help his teacher plan appropriate learning experiences for him, ones that will challenge his thinking and lead him to learn new things.

Another very significant insight from this observation has to do with Warney's articulation of certain letters. *Is Warney's language consistent with his age?* The misarticulation of letters *l* and *r* and the blend *gr* are within the range of typical articulation errors for a young four year old. Certainly the teacher would want to be aware of these but, at this point in his development, their presence is not reason for immediate concern. Warney's misarticulations are only one of the significant language clues in this episode. His generalizations related to "-est" on the end of words indicate that his is forming an age-typical characteristic.

One final word about Warney's language. As a child, *fwapes* was the term my family used when we wanted frozen grapes (one of my mother's specialties). Perhaps some of his pronunciations are typical of his family. This or some other interpretation would be more credible if Warney were articulating the letter *r* correctly in other words.

The behavior-unit anecdotal record focuses on an incident of behavior. It specializes in providing information about a child's interactions—with others, with materials, with ideas. Details are important.

"Seems to me I recollect..."
Incident Record

1. What is an incident record?

An **incident record** is a brief description that captures the essence of the behavior or episode. It has little to offer in the way of details, but may be the type of observation to start with if you are having difficulty devoting time to observing while children are in action. Because they are easy to do and simple to keep, **incident records** are a favorite tool of many observers. They can be conveniently kept using 3"x 5" index cards or sticky pads.

The **incident record** can be useful and deserves a place in your repertoire of observation tools. The picture it presents is similar to what you would get if you put your mental video recorder on fast forward and caught the behavior in generalities. Brevity is one of the important contributions of this observation tool, along with the fact that it can be recorded long after the incident has occurred. Remembering the general characteristics and the sequence of the actions is all that is needed.

2. What does an incident record look like?

Figure 19 is an example of an **incident record**. Think about the level of understanding you acquire about Lydia compared with what you learned about Warney. Is there a difference in the richness of observation data between the observations of Warney and Lydia? What factors that provide richness are missing?

Background: Lydia is a three-year-old at a small preschool with 12 children in her class.

Observable actions: Lydia arrives at school and puts things in her locker. She trots over to an activity area and starts to play with Shana and Erin. They play with the dolls for a few minutes, talking all the time. Lydia leaves the area.

Figure 19. Sample **incident record**

Clearly this **incident record** includes much less detail about Lydia than did *Figure 18*, the behavior-unit anecdotal record on Warney. The meaning of the children's behavior in an incident record is not as clear or complete as the details make possible in the behavior-unit anecdotal record.

3. When should I use an incident record?

Incident records are frequently used over a long period of time to build a file, which is why recording them on cards is so convenient. With a number of incident records, patterns in a child's behavior begin to emerge as you reread the cards. Trends in actions come into focus when enough incident cards are available for a child.

Activity Time

1. Watch for an interesting, puzzling, or significant occurrence.
2. Record the incident in a couple of sentences. (Try 3" x 5" cards or sticky notes.)
3. Keep incident records for several weeks without intentionally focusing on any child.
4. Review your cards to see if you have more than one incident record on any child. Focus on that child for several more records. Look for patterns or similarities in actions or reactions.
5. Write down what you think you have figured out about each child.

Incident records are a handy tool for recording what you remember after the fact. They are characterized by brevity and generalities. A series of records may be needed for meaning to emerge.

"Tell me about the story of..." —Narrative

1. What is a narrative observation?

The **narrative** is so named because this type of observation tells about or narrates the general story of what went on without much attention to detail. Writing a narrative is like telling a parent about a field trip or sharing with your coworker what the morning was like before she came into the classroom. Narratives are usually written in generalities, which make them very easy observation tools to use. These same qualities limit their value because of the lack of action specifics.

One potential use is to include a narrative description of a typical day in the orientation materials you share with families. If you work in a child care, preschool, or private school setting, the narrative of a typical day can be a recruiting tool to use with families who are considering placing their child in your program. Try including a brief **narrative** observation as part of your promotional materials. Remember to change the names of children included in the narrative to protect confidentiality.

2. What does a narrative look like?

The **narrative** observation in *Figure 20* describes the events for one day in the infant care area of a child care center.

> The first infant (Avera) arrived at 7:30 a.m., followed by two (Norman and Quinton) at 7:47 and a final one (Sena) at 8:10. We had only four with us for the day. A. was sleepy when she arrived and slept until 9:30. N. and Q. were awake until 8:45, when we fed them and they went down for a nap. S. arrived wide awake and played until 9:30. The morning was spent sleeping and playing, with diaper checks upon waking and frequently throughout the day. All four took at least one bottle during the morning.
>
> The morning was an easy and placid one for all four, with no significant periods of crying or upset. Each enjoyed being held and rocked in the rocking chair. All four were awake and playing at the same time for about an hour around lunch time. This was followed by diaper checks, feeding, and naps.

Figure 20. **Narrative** observation

General? Yes, but this record does present a sense of what the morning was like. As is typical of narrative observations, there is little specific information on each child other than arrival and initial action times. Also missing in this record are the infant's behaviors or cues that cause the narrative writer to say things such as "easy and placid one for all four" or "each enjoyed being held and rocked."

The narrative of a typical day can be a helpful recruiting tool to use with families.

Remember that the purpose for the narrative is to tell about rather than describe the action details. Clearly the writer of this narrative had seen certain indicators in each infant's body language that caused him to see the actions as worth recording. What he wrote is a translation of those cues into a general statement. If you are new to working with children, you might not be able to generalize the cues to reach these conclusions.

Narratives do have a place in the overall observation picture, but they are not the appropriate tool if your purpose is to gather information to understand a specific child. Narratives can be modified to provide some specifics if the observer narrows the time frame and records something about each child or chooses to focus on one child's range of activities. The example in *Figure 21* is from a preschool with four year olds.

Jon was first to arrive at 12:15 p.m. He went right to the block corner. Sierra, Enika, and Monique arrived together and went to the art area together. Burt and Jordan arrived about a minute after the girls. Burt hurried to woodworking while Jordan joined Jon in blocks. Dominika, Sheri, Calli, and Otis arrived shortly thereafter. Dominika and Calli stopped to talk with the teacher while Sheri and Otis headed to the manipulatives area. Joey, Eddie, Bruce, Buddy, and Rod tumbled into the room right after the girls. They were already planning what the turtles would do today and headed straight for the loft area. Alisa, Carrie, and Sandy arrived about three minutes later. Each had a doll with her. The three of them went to play in housekeeping. Tanika was late, arriving at about 12:45. She stood at the door for about five minutes before she slowly walked over to housekeeping and asked if she could play.

Figure 21. **Narrative** observation, specified time

This observation record is fairly general. The narrative tells the story of the first choice of activity for each child. It also provides a sense of the arrival sequence. These could be important pieces of information to have in written form.

Narratives are easy to do. If you want to practice with one, choose a period of time to write about. Free choice play time or arrival time can be good choices. Describe in general terms the events of that time period. Try to include a reference to each child. As an alternative, be more general and describe the types of things you see children doing.

3. When should I use a narrative observation?

The **narrative** observation style should be your tool of choice when you are interested in the general flow of behavior. With its many adaptations for time and scope, the narrative provides versatility. Some observers are more comfortable telling the story of events rather than writing about specifics. The narrative is a natural in this situation.

Narrative observations provide an opportunity to blend the objective actions with a subjective tone and this makes them less threatening for families to read. Because of this, the narrative is considered to be a more casual observation style.

Remember the narrative style is a flowing one, a style that tells the general story.

The narrative is the final member of the **anecdotal records** family of observation tools, and the final observation tool we explore in this chapter. The various forms of anecdotal records provide a wide range of opportunities for writing about important events in the lives of young children.

"Teacher, read it again!"
—By Way of Review

Think back over the various observation tools we explored in this chapter. With your knowledge of the strengths and challenges posed by each individual tool, you can now make an informed decision as to which tool you want to use in a particular situation. Remember that no one tool can do it all. No tool is always a better choice. Each tool has its own time and place, value and function. Your choice must be governed by the kind of information you need, your relationship with the child, and the amount of time you have available to devote to observation.

Be creative! Develop your own variation on the themes of the observation tool families. Sometimes *THE* best tool is a combination of functions from several different tools. Who knows, your own hybrid may be just what you need. You may even invent a new tool!

-Chapter Five-

On the Importance of Being Organized

In Chapter 4, we explored a number of different observation forms and recording tools. Using them regularly will yield lots of information about children. For all this information to be useful, a system is needed to bring order and organization to it. This chapter focuses on suggestions for keeping orderly, organized, and accessible records for data generated through observations.

These suggestions support optimum use of carefully observed and recorded information. Some suggestions are more helpful with certain tools, while other ideas have broader applications. Think about how these strategies might be used to organize your observation records.

Typically developing children of a given age often show levels of development as much as two years younger or older than their chronological age.

Organization of Milestones —Developing Checklists

Authentic assessment is a very important function for observation information and your observation skills. To use observations for assessment purposes, you will need more information about children. Knowing the important milestones in each area of development—the stages and accomplishments that children will achieve as they grow and develop—will give you a framework within which to analyze children's actions.

The sequence of these milestones is one organizational strategy useful for making sense of the information from observations. This sequence can become a simple checklist for any area of development (see Chapter 4). Think through what actions or behaviors indicate that a particular milestone has been reached. Comparing a child's actions with a set of established goals for her progress will provide a measure of whether or not you are helping her meet these goals.

Typically developing children of a given age often show levels of development as much as two years younger or older than their chronological age. Useful checklists need to cover this four-year age span. Begin with milestones as much as two years younger than the child being assessed and include milestones as much as two years beyond the child's age.

If the checklist is to be used with a group of children, it should include milestones representative of the least mature and the most mature children. The optimal checklist is one that is specific to the children being assessed and includes items the teacher finds relevant and useful. Checklists used in multi-age settings should span the age range of the group.

A good checklist:

- Provides a feel for the child's progress.
- Focuses on what is needed to provide for or encourage a child's progress to the next milestone.
- Is stated so there is no question about whether or not a particular action does or doesn't fit the item.

Persons who work with young children daily are in a unique position to observe children's growth and development because they spend so many hours together. In settings where teachers are with children for several years, there is an even greater potential for knowledge and understanding. Observation records help document and maintain a perspective on the child's growth during a given time period. Value your observations of children because they document the results of your hard work and efforts to nurture, care, and support the progress and growth of confident and competent, maturing young humans.

"You gotta have a system!" —Organizing Observation Records

An orderly system for maintaining observation information is the best way to ensure records can be located when needed. Information organized by individual children is the most typical and useful form. Because observation records are on individuals as well as groups, identify the significant players in each record and use these children's files as the primary location for the document. These observations also contain behavior records that may be important for understanding others in the group, so a strategy for easy recall is necessary. One answer may be to develop a **cross-reference system**, which is described in the next section of this chapter.

The system you use to organize observation findings must take into account the tools used for recording the information. For example, if observations are recorded on notebook paper, a **loose-leaf notebook** with a tabbed divider for each child makes sense. Children's records could be alphabetized or grouped according to some other characteristic, such as birth date. Observations that have the identified child as the main character would be placed behind each child's name tab. Using a cross-reference system would mean placing sheets with the name of the main character and the date behind tabs for each child mentioned in the observation but not identified as the main player.

If **sticky pad sheets** are the tool of choice for recording, the loose-leaf notebook and divider tab system also works well. Insert blank sheets behind each child's name and affix the sticky notes to the paper. Because your observations are dated, you probably will want to put them in order of occurrence. One of the advantages of using sticky pads is that they facilitate reorganization by subcategories. For example, perhaps you want to look at all the information you have on a child's social interactions. Sticky notes are easily moved and can be recombined in a category such as "social interaction" or even subcategories such as "initiates social interactions" or "responds aggressively in social interactions."

When observations are recorded on **index cards,** a file box or something that will hold them for easy view is essential. A tabbed divider for each child provides structure for organization and helps separate each child's observations. Tabbed dividers also make filing the cards easier. File observation cards behind the child's name and in order by date. Putting the newest card in the front of the stack makes a quick view of recent behavior records easy. A real advantage for using cards is that a quick glance at the thickness of the stack indicates each child's visibility. Any child who appears to be overlooked can be easily identified by the lack of cards behind his name.

A **behavior diary** or **running log** written in book form will prove difficult to organize and reorganize unless a computer is used. Organizing data by individual child requires a separate sheet of paper for each. Otherwise, entries that relate to individual children must be cut apart or rewritten in order to organize information for each child. This is time-consuming and unnecessary.

One strategy that might work is a locator key which functions like a table of contents. With this strategy, make a separate card for each child and write on the card the dates when information on each child appears in the **behavior diary** or **running log** observation. Do the same with a sheet of paper if using the notebook format. This organizational strategy helps observers tell at a glance which entries include information on a given child.

If your behavior diary or running log observations do not include records of specific behavior or records for individual children, being able to refer to them will not be a major concern. An easier approach is to use cards for keeping behavior diary or running log observation information.

"In two places at the same time?" —Information Can Be, We Can't

Frequently several children's behaviors are recorded in a single observation. Yet most teachers need to access records on a particular child rather than for the entire group. A well-developed **cross-reference system** is an efficient and easy way to pinpoint the location of information for any child in a group observation. This simple strategy maximizes the availability of information with a minimum of effort. Cross referencing eliminates the need to recopy the record for each child's file.

A cross-reference system—which identifies file locations that contain references to information for all group members—has several essential components that have to do with multiple ways to establish identification. To set up a cross-reference system:

1. Ensure that all original observations are dated.
2. Determine who the primary child is in each observation, based on the information recorded.
3. Indicate on each observation the names of children involved in the episode. A handy way to do this is to list in the top margin the names of all children mentioned.
4. Make a reference page for each child other than the primary child in the specific observation. List the name of the child (primary child) as this is where the original observation can be found. For example: "See Juan's file for 2/16." The date is just as important as the name in this cross-reference system. The date identifies which observation of Juan's to see.
5. File the original observation in the primary child's observation file.
6. File the reference copies for all children appearing in the original observation record. When information on a given child is needed, the reference copy will identify where to look without having to search through all children's observation records.

Observation Enters the Technological Age —Using a Computer

Enter the computer. For those who find it useful, a computer makes moving information on a child a snap (well, almost!). Some observers may have access to a laptop computer, and can enter their notes while they are observing. Transferring your records to computer files can be time consuming as well as an efficiency enhancer.

Just as with paper copies, the information must be organized in some manner. The most likely way to organize your files is by names of individual children. If your computer program includes search capabilities, the process of locating information on children is simplified. One computer advantage is that files can be locked to ensure confidentiality. Computers also make it possible to provide families with their own appealing-to-look-at copies of selected and edited observation data.

Using a computer is not necessary and *not* worth the time and effort unless one is readily available and its use is within your comfort zone. A computer with search capabilities would be a great help when **behavior diary** or **running log** observation tools are used, if these are entered into a computer file. Computers make possible pulling up and printing just the parts of a complete developmental checklist or other observation tool that fit the child's current level of development. These could be shared in a meaningful way with families. Computers are a tool that should simplify the task and make things easier. If that's not the case, don't use one!!

" One, two. I can buckle my shoe."
—A Progress Portfolio

One of the newest approaches in education related to the assessment of children's progress is the use of a **portfolio**. A **portfolio** is an organized set of products or other indicators of child activity or progress. Usually the items included are examples representative of the child's learning and development, such as drawings, writing samples, photographs of block constructions, stories written, and paintings. For a portfolio to serve as a valid assessment, the examples need to be systematically reviewed and evaluated to determine the child's level of progress.

Observation records can serve an important function in assessment and can become part of a child's total **portfolio**. When observations are included, they are in addition to the other information sources. A child's total education experience is best evaluated when information comes from many sources. Appropriate curriculum planning and placement decisions can be made when there is a rich source of information. The many pieces and types of information also provide teachers with valuable resources to communicate a child's progress to families. Teachers in different settings use observation records and assessments in a variety of ways based on portfolios.

No matter the setting, all who work with young children can benefit from analyzing observations of children taken over time. Good assessment data enhances:

- curriculum and management decisions
- communication with families
- placement decisions

A **progress portfolio** is also appropriate in child care, where the emphasis will probably be on the growth and development of the whole child rather than documenting learning progress. Observation records that have been thoughtfully reflected upon and that have been carefully analyzed to show a child's accomplishments related to developmental milestones are a **progress portfolio**.

Often large centers are organized into age-level classes where children move from one care giver to another. A **progress portfolio**, shared with the child's next care giver, would provide insights about how to work effectively with the child and ease the child's transition to new groups. With the family's permission, it may be wise to share the information with the child's future teachers as well.

For observations to make maximum contributions to a child's **progress portfolio**, observers need a standard or consistent approach for comparison. The first step is developing the standard. One strategy is to gather and organize information related to the appropriate milestones. Another would be to examine and use an already developed continuum or checklist. A well-thought-out **checklist** arranged in sequential order of development or acquisition of the skill makes a good beginning point of reference for a **progress portfolio**. Step two involves reflecting on what you know about the child. Document which child's products support your observations. Collect samples of children's work or take photos of their products. Step three is to analyze the information by comparing it with the standard. Step four involves organizing the information into an overall picture of the child's progress. The final step is the periodic monitoring and checking of observations and the child's work to validate progress. Compare his new products/skills with the milestones and his previous level of development.

A **progress portfolio** can be a big job! The reward is in your enhanced understanding of each child. Teachers who put forth the effort will know better what to plan, what help a child needs, as well as have very real and meaningful information to share with families.

Sharing Observations With Families

Complete and meaningful observation records provide teachers with information they can use to build relationships with families, relationships that enhance a child's development and learning. Sharing information with each child's family enhances your partnership with them. The child's triumphs and accomplishments are valuable assets to share with the child's family. When you do this, are families pleased and, perhaps, impressed to hear about their child's day?

Sharing a child's problems, difficulties, or areas of need identified from observations is a more sensitive situation. Few people, especially families, welcome hearing about these important issues. Identifying them for families requires great tact on the part of teachers.

However, when good dialogue occurs about areas of need, problems, or difficulty, families and teachers can come to terms with how best to support a child's healthy growth. Objective observations, recorded over a period of time, provide important documentation, should a parent be reluctant to accept realities. Even so, sensitive areas are challenging.

Activity Time

1. Identify something from your observations to share with a child's family.
2. Set up a time to meet and talk together. Be sure to discuss their perspectives of the child.
3. Ask them how they feel about sharing so many insights about their child. If their response was positive, think about how your observation skills influenced the reaction. If the response was negative, try to assess why. Would more, or more detailed, observation data have helped?

Families and teachers differ in the degree of objectivity each brings to working with a child. Teachers focus attention on, see, and know about many children. Families see and know most about their own child. Teachers with good observation information can help families see new and different capacities in their children, just as families can provide teachers with important insights about their children.

Although the purpose for observation is not to compare one child with another, the teacher's knowledge of typical child development and her objective perspective is especially valuable when a child's progress is considerably different from that of his peers. Good, objective records of a child's actions are essential to help families and perhaps other education professionals understand what you, the teacher, see in the child's progress.

"Now what do I do with them?" —Confidentiality and Storage

Observation records quickly accumulate. The problem of what to do with them, and how or where to store them, will arise. Your solution depends a lot on your teaching situation. Original copies of observations may not have much meaning to others. Young children grow and change right before our eyes. After an observation has been analyzed and the information used to enhance your effectiveness with a child, its usefulness may be over.

Keep in mind, however, that information obtained through observation should be kept confidential. Whether to share it with families or not, and how much of it to share, is up to the observer. Information must never be accessible to any one who just happens by. Check with your supervisor about what to do with observations. You may want to suggest that record-storage procedures be developed. Otherwise, it is up to you to determine what procedures are appropriate.

How long should observation records be kept? There is no standard answer. If a child is no longer in your care, there may be little need to keep records. Check your program's policies and procedures. If you are the decision maker, it is up to you to establish a policy to address the question.

"Teacher, read it again!" —By Way of Review

A system to organize information obtained by direct observation of children is a must. Easy-to-locate information is more likely to be used. Cross-reference strategies are a short cut to efficient organization of information. Observation records can be included as part of a child's progress portfolio. Keeping a progress portfolio is important, but its contents also need to be looked at and reviewed periodically. Organized observation records provide usable information when conferring with families about a child's progress and will help you and other nurturing adults recognize the progress the child is making.

-Chapter Six-

**Come to know each child as a
unique individual, to understand
each one as a person.**

Observation Dividends:
What's in it for me?

This last chapter summarizes some of the many benefits that good observation skills offer teachers. Our work with young children is enhanced by careful observation and sensitivity to each child's needs and humanness.

Careful, sensitive observation will help teachers:

- Come to know each child as a unique individual, to understand each one as a person.

- Focus on each child's specific needs. Observation helps identify the common needs of a given age group as well as variations among individuals within an age group.

- Develop insight and make decisions regarding more effective ways to work with and relate to each child. Based on individual children's reactions to the world, appropriate, sensitive responses for nurturing learning and development will emerge. Observation used for this purpose helps teachers evaluate the effectiveness of their actions as well as provide insight into how these actions influence children.

- Engage in authentic assessment of children's skills and abilities—assessments of what each child *CAN* do. Observation spotlights how a child's skills and capabilities come together to support the development of a competent, functioning person. Carefully recorded observations present these skills and capabilities in the context of how the child uses them. This real information about the child helps teachers understand how to create a meaningful learning environment and curriculum.